Better Answers

*Written Performance
That Looks Good
and Sounds Smart*

Ardith Davis Cole

Stenhouse Publishers
Portland, Maine

Stenhouse Publishers
www.stenhouse.com

Library of Congress Cataloging-in-Publication Data
Cole, Ardith Davis.
    Better answers : written performance that looks good and sounds smart / Ardith Davis Cole.
    p. cm.
    Includes bibliographical references (p.).
    ISBN 1-57110-341-4 (alk. paper)
    1. Language arts (Elementary)—United States. 2. Language arts (Middle school)—United States. 3. Test-taking skills—Study and teaching (Elementary)—United States. 4. Test-taking skills—Study and teaching (Middle school)—United States. I. Title.
LB1576.C764 2002
372.6'0973—dc21   2002017596

Cover photograph by the author

Manufactured in the United States of America on acid-free paper
07 06 05 04 03 02 9 8 7 6 5 4 3 2 1

*This book is dedicated to
my children, Brad, Jen, and Heather
and
my grandchildren, Cameron and Delanie—
all of whom continue to give me lots of practice
in constructing "better answers" to their
ongoing questions.*

Contents

Preface

High-stakes testing has radically altered the kind of instruction that is offered in American schools, to the point that "teaching to the test" has become a prominent part of the nation's educational landscape. . . . Indeed, both the content and the format of instruction are affected; the test essentially becomes the curriculum. . . . This has aptly been called the "dumbing down" of instruction.

(Kohn 2000, p. 29)

Is This Another Test-Prep Book?

This book *is* related to preparing students for written responses on assessments; so indeed, from that perspective it is "test prep." It is different, however, from the disconnected, test-prep workbook approaches that are being assigned daily throughout this nation. Using very easy text, this book helps teachers demonstrate the written response process in a step-by-step developmental manner. As soon as the process is in place, it will support all school subjects—anytime, anywhere students are asked to construct a brief or extended written response, that is, an essay.

I hope this book helps teachers and kids see response writing in a new light—one that prepares readers and writers not only for tests, but more important, for what comes after school. For adults use response writing practically every day, and we want students to be prepared for those uses. For example, skilled response writers write to their congressperson to state their stance and implore the politician to consider the relevant evidence they provide. Skilled response writers are able to construct a powerful, provoking letter to a company that has sold them a faulty product. Skilled response writers can construct memos and reports for their bosses, providing the right quantity and kind of information. Writing a test response is only a very small part of this lifelong skill.

With this in mind, this book first teaches steps that will help students construct acceptable written test responses, steps that begin a lifelong journey into better responses.

A Change in Testing

It is somewhat strange that I should write a book about anything involving tests, because I have always found such tasks to be an infringement on students' rights. Tests began to get under my skin about twenty years ago when I was teaching elementary school. With all good intention, I excluded a child, who had no understanding of print, from the sections of the IOWA test battery that assessed reading. I received a reprimand, was told that the district needed that evidence in order to get funding, and warned that I must test all children forevermore. So, the following year I gave the full battery to all my students, even a child who was later identified as mentally retarded. As it turned out, that child, who could read only a few words, bubbled in all the little circles and scored almost a second-grade level in reading. (I might better have had her fill in a lottery ticket!) Needless to say, testing continues to bother me, but not nearly so much as it used to.

Not all of today's tests resemble those of two decades past. Today many states really do have sound assessments driven by standards that if implemented with passion, interesting materials, sound methodologies, and authentic activities, will prepare students to score better than ever—in school and in life. As New York State Commissioner of Education Mills and Chancellor Hayden explain, the key is "'teaching to the standards,' not the tests," (Saunders 2001, p. 4).

Regardless, there will always be some students who will have grave problems meeting the standards, that is, kids who need special instruction and extra monitoring. Helping these students has been my main job for the past several years, and with it came the groundwork for this book.

Up to Our Elbows in Standards and Performance Assessment

By the time the standards and assessment movement had taken shape in the late 1990s I had become the reading teacher at a K–5 elementary school. That position encompassed many test-related responsibilities, of which one of the most demanding was trying to bring lower-achieving readers and writers up to snuff before "T-Day" at the end of each year. At first I was fairly confident about our students' progress because we worked very hard on reading, and most kids were able to decode by fourth grade, when T-Day arrives for New York State students—and teachers.

Furthermore, I was quite familiar with the state expectations and documents. Throughout the period that New York was developing its English Language Arts Standards and Assessments, professional organizations and teachers were invited to participate with the Department of Education. I had the good fortune of being a member of the New York State Reading Association's governing board at that time, and was very involved in the process. I knew that these new English Language Arts Standards rested on sound constructivist research and were authentically related to real-life tasks; so, I was confident in their implementation. In fact, as I surfed the Net I was happy to see that many other states had standards and assessments similar to those of New York. We all seemed to be moving toward a constructivist perspective; thus, my outlook on testing began to take a positive turn.

Panic Sets In

I did not expect the reaction that occurred after the first tests were given and the results were published in newspapers across the state. Everyone panicked! Everything had changed, but not in a way that I could have ever predicted.

For one thing, teachers were taken aback by the new test format. That is, educators in our state and other states (e.g., Florida, Kentucky, California, New Jersey, Maryland, Georgia, Delaware, Michigan, South Carolina, and Indiana) were surprised by the quantity of brief and extended responses required in the assessments. No longer are there just simplistic tasks that call for students to read and bubble in answers to multiple-choice questions. Now, students have to also construct short and extended written responses to complex, multifaceted questions. One answer can have several parts, and students must use detailed evidence from the text to support their statements. Plus, they have to write cohesively, coherently, and correctly. In all subjects! This is no small challenge—for kids or for those in charge of their instruction.

Literacy Specialist, Fix Them!

The pressure was exacerbated by new state mandates regarding interventions for students who did not meet standards on the grade 4, 8, and 11 English Language Arts Assessments. We had our work cut out for us: Creative and sensible interventions had to be developed to help our struggling students. For me, the real crunch came when I was presented with the list of fifth-grade students who had not met the ELA standards on the grade 4 state assessment, and was then asked to develop an intervention that would help them as quickly as possible to meet the required standards.

Most of these students had been receiving reading interventions for years. They had participated in summer programs and several other special intervention protocols to support their growth, which had been carefully monitored throughout. I had spreadsheets to show they had been continually progressing. Yet, they did not meet the standard. What else could I do?

I knew I would not have a daily period to work with these students. They could not miss important classroom instruction and experiences, nor could they be asked to give up after-school music, sports, and scouts. What could I possibly do in two periods per week that had not already been done?

A Protocol That Worked

I began by reviewing the state assessment and investigating the answers each student had constructed. During this process a protocol began to take shape, with my number one goal being to teach these students how to construct an essay answer. I also realized that constructing a sound answer to a question is a life skill beyond the classroom. It is something we must do in both formal and informal situations throughout our daily lives, for example, to apply for a job or give directions to a lost driver. With this twofold objective in mind, I set out to develop a protocol that would help the students perform well on short or extended-response educational assessments, as well as when they encounter questions in their out-of-school lives. This was the beginning of the Better Answers formula.

With the support of their classroom teachers, the process worked! Within only four months, ten of the eighteen intervention students had met the grade 5 English Language Arts Standards. Those results, as well as the students' positive responses to the protocol, prompted me to share the strategies with others.

In early 2001 I presented a "Better Answers" workshop to grade 4 and 8 teachers at School 45 in Buffalo and then went into their classrooms to do demos. They continued to reinforce those demos, and months later, when the two grade levels received the results of that year's state English Language Arts Assessment, one of their teachers was so excited that she sat down and wrote me a letter. Denise Vassar knew I was writing this book, and she asked me to share her good news with you. She wrote: "This is the first year I had students score a 4 [the highest score]! My students scored 2s, 3s, and 4s (no 1s), an overall improvement from last year. The struggling readers who were in the 1 zone scored a 2 and I know that's because of [the

Better Answer Formula and note-taking tips]. . . . When you make learning fun and interesting and show confidence in their ability to learn, the students will make every effort to do their best."

I am pleased to share Denise's good news. However, we both know that constructing a test answer is not enough for our kids. We want them to develop meaningful essays connected to the real world—essays with voice, intention, and focus. Teachers who connect this protocol to authentic situations in the real world will have students who will blow the top off any essay test put before them. They will also be able to function optimally in their careers; better answers are not composed only on tests.

An Invitation

I invite you and your students to try the Better Answer protocol. I sincerely hope that you will then be able to throw those test-prep workbooks into the recycling bin, and instead use Better Answer techniques not only in language arts, but also in science, social studies, literature—indeed, all school subjects.

Acknowledgments

First and foremost, I wish to thank the students in whose classrooms I constructed and implemented various phases of the Better Answer formula: the group of fifth graders from Maplemere Elementary School in Amherst, New York, who walked with me as I stumbled and bumbled my way through the first leg of this journey; the kids in grades 3, 4 and 8 at Buffalo's International School 45 who helped me shade and hue the protocol to accommodate a multitude of individual differences; the kids in Barb McKay's fourth grade, who amongst other things, even lent a hand in creating the book's assessment samples; and all those others in the city of Buffalo and Sweet Home, each of whom added a small piece to this whole. Furthermore, a very special thanks goes to the fourth graders from Buffalo Schools 45 and 4, for it is their beautiful faces that grace this book.

Heartfelt thanks also go to several colleagues: Maplemere fourth-grade teacher Barb McKay, whose open door and mindful questions continue to draw me in; the principal of School 45, Colleen Caroda, who so graciously invited me into their community; Curriculum Director at School 45, Mary Ann Hopfer, my Better Answer cheerleader, who pours into my cup until my confidence runs right over the edge; the fourth-grade teachers at School 45 and School 4, Denise Vassar, Gwen Humphrey, Darlene McFadden, Maria Fasolino, and Mary Weiss, who are now "the pros"; and Lockport Middle School English teacher Renee Knight, who so graciously responded to my first draft (which was a lot longer!). What wonderful colleagues!

And of course, a big celebration hug goes to my family and friends: to Elaine Garan, who is always there and never minds hearing drafts read over the phone; to Norma Gentner, who would send the formula to everyone if she could; and to my own children and their families, who give me the inspiration, confidence, and love that all writers need.

I also want to offer a "hindsight" thank you to Anne Fullerton, who edited my first book and from whom I learned more than any writing course could ever teach. I think of Anne again and again, as her knowledgeable guidance continues to guide my pen.

And last, but certainly not least, I want to extend my sincere appreciation to the helpful and patient individuals at Stenhouse Publishers: to Philippa Stratton, who immediately believed in Better Answers and, along with the reviewers of the early draft, gave direction and focus for this final product; to Tom Seavey, a longtime professional friend; and to Martha Drury, who walked me through the final stages of the journey. These individuals helped me to see the manuscript through a different lens, and because of them its final incarnation is a far better product. For that, I am grateful.

My gratitude also goes to you, the reader, who decided to try the protocol on for size. May your own journey into better answers be as exciting and rewarding an experience as mine has been.

Introduction to the Better Answer Formula

Writing makes us better teachers. When our students see how we struggle, organize, think, reread, revise, edit, and get ideas with and through our own writing, they are supported in their writing. When they see our process—because we show it to them, speak it aloud, do it in front of them—we are demonstrating the most powerful of practices while giving them a lifelong gift and tool.

(Routman 1996, p. 183)

During my first year of teaching in 1964 I took some of my first graders' writing samples to share with other teachers at a district grade-level meeting. To my dismay, these new colleagues were appalled. "You gave your students a pencil?" they exclaimed. "You are not supposed to give first graders pencils until second semester!"

Times have certainly changed since the days of Dick and Jane lessons and color-the-bubble tests. Today's kids are writing their life stories on journal pages in grade 1, reading chapter books by grade 2, and collaborating as researchers by grade 3. Along with all these changes has come a new way of thinking about test tasks. In most states, by the time students exit grade 3 they are expected to be able to construct brief and extended essay responses to questions related to a variety of content presented through listening and/or reading. I wonder what those 1964 grade 1 teachers would say about that!

In some cases, changes have happened so quickly that they have left us teachers breathless and filled with anxieties. Reading a brief passage and then selecting one of four given answers is very different from what students must do on the tests of the twenty-first century. Students of the past who could read did not have to be able to write to score well on district and state reading tests. They merely had to color in bubbles or encircle letters or phrases. When a child's reading is assessed through his or her writing, it adds a whole new dimension to testing. We have moved students from recall to restate to respond and reflect—a mighty task for all concerned.

Just how mighty this task was became clear when my school was notified of the students who had not met the standards on the grade 4 state literacy assessment. Because I was asked to bring the eighteen students up to proficiency level, as soon as their tests were returned to us, I investigated the performance of those eighteen students with a fine-tooth comb. It wasn't long before commonalities in their responses emerged. Enter the Better Answer formula.

The Better Answer Formula
Strategy 1: Restate the question.
Strategy 2: Construct a gist answer.
Strategy 3: Use details to support your answer.
Strategy 4: Stay on the topic.
Strategy 5: Use proper conventions.

The first thing I noticed was that many students did not seem to even know what the question was. They appeared to have answered a different question! Thus, Step 1 began to take shape: Ask them to simply restate the question.

Next I noticed how shallow their responses were. Some students wrote little more than one sentence. I had often heard teachers suggest, "Write more," but it never worked. This problem took awhile to solve; I did not conceive of Step 2 until we had stumbled and bumbled our way through many fruitless possibilities. Finally, I realized that an answer had to first be only a general, or gist, response (Step 2), which would then be followed by the details to support that initial general answer (Step 3). Essentially, Step 1 led into Step 2, which made Step 3 easier, because it provided a specific pathway to the details.

Everything seemed to be going well until the students got carried away with the details. This brought about Step 4, which demonstrates how to stay on the topic. Eventually, it was obvious that their previously shallow responses had grown into sound content. Yet, handwriting, smudges, spelling, grammar, and other aspects of readableness were still taking their toll. Therefore, Step 5, related to conventions, took root and grew into a productive counterpart. Over months and years the Better Answer formula was refined and extended to include numerous concrete supports, such as the Answer Sandwich and the Answer Scale, which are included in this book.

Of the five steps in the process, the first four are related to the *content* of the response, and the last one focuses on the *presentation* of that content, that is, the conventions, handwriting, and neatness. As research has suggested again and again, our first priority in any piece of writing is its content. With that in place, its surface features become the final concern. Five steps to success!

A Developmental Model Leads to Success

The Better Answer technique is a developmental model, with each step building on the previous one. The first step is so easy that even struggling students establish a level of confidence. Each step becomes more difficult, but each evolves out of the previous one, producing a kind of scaffolding effect. This, along with all of the concrete organizers and other supports, helps students slide from Step 1 through Step 5 and into success.

That success could be seen on the faces of those fifth graders I mentioned earlier! Their smiles reflected the pride that resulted from being able to construct a sound and acceptable written response. In the end, seeing that pride and their new level of confidence was the greatest payoff.

I have since used this protocol with learners at several other levels in grades 3 through 8, including inner-city students identified as special education and ESL. When implemented step by step with lots of modeling, it works to raise levels of literacy performance on brief and extended, or essay, responses with students across grade levels. It has even worked for adults!

Simplifying a Complicated Process

Almost everything we learn begins with baby steps. We practice golfing behaviors at the driving range and the putting green before we attempt eighteen holes. Children use training wheels, as Mom or Dad hangs onto the seat, before they ride bicycles independently across town to a friend's house. We learn to swim in three feet of water, not the deep end of the pool. Anytime children or adults are learning a new task, it is made easier by eliminating the variables that might distract, frighten, or confuse them.

Considering this, I decided that students would probably learn the steps in this process more easily and more confidently if we initially used simplistic text. Why complicate matters! That assumption proved correct—even for teachers learning the process in workshops! Old, well-known tales, such as "Little Red Riding Hood," are the grist for each strategy's modeling sessions and for the students' first attempts at using the strategy. These familiar tales create the perfect background for success in learning response techniques, because novices do not have to wade through tough text while learning a new strategy. We remove that burden, so they can concentrate on the process itself. Old tales become our driving range and putting green, anchors to be referenced again and again.

Most children are familiar with old tales such as "Little Red Riding Hood" and "The Three Little Pigs"; yet, it is still important to read a version of each story before using it. We can never assume that everyone in the group knows these tales, even though many are found in cultures across the world. Furthermore, because the Better Answer process works effectively with both nonfiction and fiction, using these fictional tales does not deter the transfer to more difficult, nonfiction text later. The same steps—the same process—are used for any brief, extended, or essay response. As a matter of fact, the process works just as well in the real world, on the job or wherever written response occurs.

A Baseline Assessment

I usually suggest that teachers use one of the samples included Appendix A to obtain a baseline assessment before beginning the protocol. The longer samples work well for grades 5 through 8, and the shorter ones for grades 3 and 4. I ask teachers to simply read one of the tales aloud to their students, afterward asking them to respond to one of my question or petition prompts (also in the appendix). We then tuck these pre-assessments away.

When we finish teaching the entire formula, we do a post-assessment in the same manner, but using another of the provided tales. Then, we evaluate both the pre- and the post-assessments using the rubric in Chapter 3. Appendix E contains examples of spreadsheets for monitoring such individual and class progress, which will not only provide the present waystation at which each student resides, but also will show quite clearly the progress he or she has made since the beginning of the Better Answer journey.

The best part of this experience, however, is sharing the results with our kids. My own students (that first year) could not believe how they had improved. Every one of them! What a confidence builder it was!

Modeling Is Mandatory

You'll quickly notice that each step is introduced through modeling, think-alouds, and shared writing experiences. Stephanie Harvey (1998) calls these initial, supported, memorable experiences "anchoring," because each can remain a common reference experience for the whole class. Therefore, it is quite usual to hear a teacher say something like, "Remember when we developed an answer to that 'Three Little Pigs' question? How did we do the details then?" Such anchors become important supports during the process.

Furthermore, students need to observe how we teachers think and compose in order to emulate those behaviors. For students to reenact our moves and thoughts, they need to understand how we wind our way, step by step, through a process. Learning is scaffolded down an avenue of success when we take the onus off the learners, allowing them to just listen and learn without the threat of "doing it wrong" hanging over them.

I especially like to demonstrate that the act of writing is not a neat and tidy process, that sometimes things get pretty jumbled and we must drop back and press our restart buttons. Modeling is probably the most important aspect of this entire instructional process—the one thing that should never be omitted. When students are not doing well, I know it is usually because I did not model enough.

No matter what the grade level is, I try to teach each new important concept using the following sequence.

A Scaffolded Instructional Framework
- Teacher models Task A (for example, Step 1), while students watch and listen.
- Teacher gradually invites students in through partnering (dyads).
- Teacher invites students into larger groups.
- Students work independently on Task A.
- Teacher continues to scaffold students gradually toward a more skilled Task A performance.

Certainly, constructing a written response is not the only skill in life that is better learned through this kind of scaffolded instruction. It's a basic confidence builder, and without confidence it is tough to look good and sound smart.

Lookin' Good! Soundin' Smart!

One of the essential things that I want kids to know is that their entire performance is about lookin' good and soundin' smart. There are definitely times throughout life when we need to look good and sound smart. Taking tests in school is only one of those times.

We also need to look good and sound smart at job interviews, on college and employment applications, when speaking with a high official, when being interviewed before the public, or when attempting to explain why we want our money back on broken merchandise. Indeed, there are many times in life when it is important to use formal language and to present ourselves in a somewhat different manner than we do at home with our family and friends. At such times, we change the register of our language. And so it should be.

The Better Answer formula will help students do this. It will help them look good and sound smart.

What's Inside?

Vignettes, Activities, and Resources

Each chapter begins by describing how to model a particular step of the protocol for the students. Examples and samples can be transferred right out of the book and into the classroom. This book contains examples I have used a gazillion times—and am still using. Readers will also find classroom vignettes that provide a bird's-eye view of how each step plays out during a lesson. Steps 1 and 2 are presented together through a vignette toward the end of Chapter 2; and Steps 3 and 4 are presented via vignette after Chapter 4. These "written movies" will help to internalize the process.

The complementary activities interspersed throughout will provide review, reinforcement, or extension of the presented strategies. For some steps in the process, the activities will be necessary for reinforcement because students need more practice. When students appear to have conquered a particular step fairly easily, the review or extension activities will serve as a different kind of resource. Some activities connect to content-area learning and help students transfer parts of the formula to specific subjects. They extend the process. This variety of options can become a welcome resource in most any grade 3 through 8 classroom.

The appendixes of this book provide a head start into the process; they are chockful of handy supports—everything from lesson plans, to text samples, to a bibliography of resources. So before implementing, it would be a good idea to just leaf through that last part of the book to see how it can save you time and trouble.

Real-World Connections

This book also contains continual references to real-world response writing, because the Better Answer formula serves multiple purposes well—both in and out of school. As a matter of fact, our ultimate teaching intentions should *not* be limited to right answers on tests. Our ultimate intentions should connect such learning to the privileges and rights of committed citizens in a democratic society. Essentially, that is what response writing is all about. It's about making one's voice heard, evoking change, and forging pathways to a better world. Therefore, watch for places where such connections can be made—not only my suggested connections, but any real-world seeds that can be planted. Through these meaningful applications students develop the greatest intention to learn.

How Long Will This Take?

Many teachers ask about the length of time needed for implementation of this protocol. Obviously, it will vary according to age, ability, and background level of the students involved. I have taught Steps 1 and 2 in a single lesson, and the kids exited looking like pros. But, it has also taken a week for some students to internalize Steps 1 and 2. Integration across the curriculum definitely makes a difference, though; the more students experience the protocol, the more rapid the internalization. However, continual attention to the Assessing and Conferring sections in each chapter will be one of the greatest supports in predicting the answer to "How long will this take?"

Assessing and Conferring

Assessing and conferring are presented in tandem because one grows out of the other; that is, we teachers continually assess where a student is, and then we do something to take him or her to the next level—through either a spoken or a written communication or conference. For instance, we notice the student is not restating the question or is not indenting; so we provide the instructional nudge it will take for that child to move forward. To support such individual assistance, the Assessing and Conferring sections provide a relevant type of assessment for that particular plateau, followed by some strategic questions to undergird those nudges. The better we know our students (assessing), the faster we can help them (conferring) get where they're going.

Dump the Test-Prep Workbooks!

One thing is sure! There will be a whole lot more time in the day once the Better Answer formula replaces those test-prep workbooks. After the formula is understood, it will integrate right into any curriculum—science, social studies, math, technology, or literature.

In contrast, test-prep workbooks are a curriculum in and of themselves. They usurp a considerable amount of time, and yet they are not easy to integrate. For one thing, they are boring! Additionally, their narratives and text pieces are not related to our curriculum; they are related to what the test manufacturer has in mind—entities unto themselves; that is, they apply only to tests. On the other hand, this formula is applicable across the curriculum—anywhere that questions are asked and answers are developed.

The Ground Floor

The Better Answer formula is the beginning of a never-ending journey to becoming a better response writer. It is a foundation, a ground floor. Its fundamental strategies and simplicity build the confidence to move into more complex, yet similar tasks—tasks that will be required both in school and throughout life.

Let's see how it works.

Restate the Question

If the language we use in the classroom is not the same as the language we use in real life, surely we are wasting valuable time.

(Fox 1993, p. 68)

Restating: A Real-World Skill

Restating the question happens to be the easiest step, but it is also probably the most important step in the process because it gets the writer off on the right foot. Furthermore, this is not just a school skill. In real life (as compared with school life) people use restating to give themselves another minute to think about the answer and confirm that they have indeed understood the request.

Restating also makes people sound smart, articulate. Not long ago I was listening to "Science Friday" on National Public Radio. Ira Flatow was interviewing a notable scientist, and each time he asked that scientist a question, the scientist began his answer by restating the interviewer's question. He restated it every time! This is something that good communicators do in real life, especially when they want to look good and sound smart. And, that is exactly what I tell students.

Restating: A Portal to the Answer

Restating also becomes a portal to the answer; that is, it leads the restater more naturally toward the next step, which is the answer. I noticed when I surveyed the grade 4 students' brief and extended responses from their state assessments that many times they did not have the correct answer because *they did not appear to know what the question was*. It often sounded like the writer was beginning in the middle of nowhere, and although he was somewhere, it was not usually where the answer was. But, when a responder begins with a restatement that uses the question's words, it locates him exactly where he should be.

This is why I begin with restating, considering it a fundamental step in the process. Let's investigate how we can lay this groundwork; once this step is in place, the next unfolds quite naturally.

Teaching Avenues for Restating

Modeling That Uses Personal Questions

I begin Step 1 by discussing what it means to restate a question, but I soften the process by using personal rather than text-related questions. Obviously, kids are more interested in personal matters; plus, it tends to keep meaning front and center within a parroting process. For instance, I often show students how to restate the question, "What did you do last night when you got home from school?"

One word of caution when constructing those first demonstration questions: Make certain your example is the kind of question that calls for a somewhat extended response, one we will later call a "thick question." We're trying to avoid yes and no answers, because we will use these questions again in Steps 2 and 3 of the formula. It's also wise to save all the restatement charts constructed during this step; it will eliminate redoing Step 1 when entering Step 2.

I begin by discussing ways to restate sample questions. Some examples of such personal, extended-response questions include

- What did you do last night when you got home from school?
- Why is it important to be on time for school every day?
- How do the members of your family enjoy free time together?
- What do people do to take good care of their pets?
- If you did not know a friend's phone number, how might you find it?

Open-Ended and Closed Restatements

It's important to note that questions can be restated in two ways: open-ended and closed. Open-ended restatements end without closure, and usually with a transition word, such as *because*. Using the personal questions just listed, I model a couple of open-ended restatements for the students, and then invite them into the process. This beginning part is all oral, and we do not at this time move on to the answer.

Using the sample questions, open restatements might sound like the following example.

Open Restatements
- Last night when I got home from school I . . . (no transition term)
- It is important to be on time for school every day to . . . (contains the transition *to*)
- The members of my family enjoy free time together by . . . (contains the transition *by*)

Sometimes a question is constructed in a manner that lends itself to a closed restatement. That is, although the words from the question are restated, that restatement becomes a complete sentence.

When I teach this second way to construct a restatement, I often say, "Period!" at the end of each restatement. In this way I am emphasizing what students' ears are telling them. Some examples of closed restatements follow.

Closed Restatements
- Last night when I got home from school I did several things.
- There are many reasons why it is important to be on time for school every day.
- The members of my family enjoy free time together in a number of ways.

Quite frequently, content-area assessment contains questions that may be appropriately answered with a closed restatement, so it's important that students understand that either way can serve their needs. Content-area questions often call for steps or lists. Consequently, during the day when these subjects are taught, it reinforces the process if attention is drawn to any restatements that can be evoked by questions that may come up.

Some closed content-area restatements follow. The questions that evoked these restatements are obvious.

Closed Restatements from Content Study

- The United States was involved in several wars in the twentieth century.
- The scientific process consists of several steps.
- This mathematical problem can be solved in two ways.
- There is much to be learned from the manner in which the first Americans grew and harvested their food.

Clearly, as long as a student restates the question, it does not matter whether that restatement is open-ended or closed. With that said, I must add that transitional, open-ended restatements probably slide their creator into the answer more easily. Ending with words like *because* and *by* just naturally call for an answer—a bit like ending a tune on a subdominant note. We can't rest until we hear what comes next.

The following examples show how open and closed restatements can be used for the same question. It might be interesting to ask students which restatement they think works better; that is, which one makes the writer look better and sound smarter. Note that at this point it is not necessary to have read the story. We are just reusing the question's words.

Questions and Restatements

- Why did Little Red Riding Hood think the character in the bed was not her grandmother?
    Open: Little Red Riding Hood did not think the character in the bed was her grandmother because . . .
    Closed: Little Red Riding Hood did not think the character in the bed was her grandmother.
- Why did Jack climb the beanstalk to the giant's castle?
    Open: Jack climbed the beanstalk to the giant's castle to . . .
    Closed: There were several reasons why Jack climbed the beanstalk to the giant's castle.
- How did the three little pigs escape from the big bad wolf?
    Open: The three little pigs escaped from the big bad wolf by . . .
    Closed: The ways that the three little pigs escaped from the big bad wolf were very clever.

After we've played with multiple ways to just restate a variety of questions, first personal and then others, we move into the written mode. I initially demonstrate how it helps to mark off the question's words as they are used in the restatement. We can then scribe from those words to construct our restatement.

Marking Words Used in the Question

Again I begin with personal questions, then move on to others related to simple fairy tales and fables. This time I prepare the students for the experience by first reading to them a brief version of a tale from which I have created several questions that would require extended answers. Beforehand I place each of these questions on a *separate* transparency or chart page, leaving room for the answers that will be developed in the course of the protocol.

Using the first question on the chart, I demonstrate how the idea works. That is, as I am restating the question, I am underlining the words that I restate, crossing out words, and writing substitutions above the crossed-out words. The substitutions or changes happen most frequently with verbs and pronouns, which must be changed in the restating to have the writing make sense and sound syntactically acceptable. I find that this crossing out and substituting is especially important for ESL and special education students, who might not readily make such changes.

I make it very clear that I think it's important to use as many of the words in the question as possible. Often, students who have used only a few of the question's words have constructed answers that are slightly or completely off-base. Therefore, we work hard to get as many of those words in our restatements as possible.

Furthermore, the specific word match discourages students from substituting pronouns for nouns, a very common practice that confuses those who read the answer later. For instance, if we asked, "Why did the wicked stepmother think Snow White was still alive?" it is common practice for students to construct restatements such as "She thought she was still alive because . . ."

To discourage that use of pronouns in introductory sentences, I make a large chart of the most common (subjective) pronouns. Then I put a slash across the chart, similar to the "No smoking" sign. It looks like this:

Verb tenses sometimes confuse students because verbs tend to change in the restatement. To help students further understand the process, I show them how we must change the verb tense, by slashing and overwriting. For instance, in the following sentence we substituted "thought" for "think" by crossing out "think" and writing "thought" above it.

<blockquote>
Why did <u>the</u> <u>wicked</u> <u>stepmother</u> <s>think</s> ^{thought} <u>Snow</u> <u>White</u> <u>was</u> <u>still</u> <u>alive</u>? (because . . .)
</blockquote>

Scribing the Restatement

After I have completed the oral restatement and the marking, I scribe that restatement below the question on the chart. When scribing restatements, it's wise to keep introductory sentences, or partial sentences, spaced out on a chart or transparency so that when you move on to Steps 2 and 3 you can return to these previously composed restatements. This eliminates extra work; it is a step that has already been done. It also serves as a ready and observable review or anchor for Step 1.

Another element that works well when incorporated into an open-ended restatement is the *ellipsis*, that is, the three sequenced dots that mean *more is to come*. Because we are not yet completing the restatement sentence with its answer, but instead leaving it open, the ellipsis becomes a perfect placeholder. I might warn, however, that many students develop a love affair with those three little dots and want to leave them there—even after the rest of the sentence has been constructed! Yet, ellipses serve their purpose well, for the ellipsis becomes a concrete "ta-da-a-a-a"—fanfare—as it calls forth the answer.

The Students' Turn to Restate Using Questions' Words

After modeling once or twice, I invite the students to come up and do the underlining, the slashing, and the substituting, as their classmates offer restatement suggestions for each page's question. When it's their turn to try out the process, I make a really big deal out of students whose restatements use almost every word in the question.

Basically, it's important for students to know that there is more than one right way to construct an answer on a performance assessment. So I extend multiple invitations to restate the same question in different ways. Such second and third versions can be scribed in another location, so that the chart remains open for the eventual answers.

I like to use these sample pages from demonstrations as wall charts. I have also developed a list of sample restatements with their transitions that can be a ready reference, as well. I like to underline the transitions, so that students become familiar with the options. Some past examples included the following.

Restatements with Transitions
- Little Red Riding Hood was not afraid of the wolf <u>because</u> . . .
- The wolf ran to Grandmother's house <u>to</u> . . .
- Father got rid of the wolf <u>by</u> . . .
- Little Red Riding Hood was afraid <u>when</u> . . .
- Little Red Riding Hood would not have been bothered by the wolf <u>if</u> . . .
- Little Red Riding Hood did not leave for Grandmother's house <u>until</u> . . .

Partner Collaboration

With all of these modeled experiences under their belts, students are ready to collaborate with a partner in constructing restatements. So, I read a short tale, after which I distribute a few questions to each dyad. Partners then "share the pen" as they take turns restating, marking, and scribing their restatements. I cruise the class as they work, observing and supporting.

After they use teacher-constructed questions, it's fun for students to create their own questions for a common fairy tale. The Better Question Menu (see Figure 6 in Chapter 3) gives the students a broad range of question options. Posting this menu on the wall allows students access to it when they are creating questions. They like the idea of having plenty of options—options that in the long run help them internalize the codependent relationship of questions and their answers.

Later, they can share with a partner, restating each other's questions. It is also fun for the students (and much like a television game show) to guess what the *question* might have been, when given only the *restatement*. Keeping this first step playful and easy is important. It captures the students' interest and grounds the process in a positive perspective.

Initially, partners tend to roll right into the answer, because it's interesting to them and they want to share it with their classmate. When I hear someone flow from the restatement right on into the answer, however, to add a spark of levity, I dash over and make a referee timeout sign with my hands, usually accompanied by, "No, no, no! No answers! Just restatements!" This creates a giggle or two; underneath it all I would speculate that they are thinking, "A teacher who *doesn't* want answers!"

Before we leave Step 1, one other item needs to be addressed that can sometimes appear as a source of confusion for the students. That item is the petition.

Petitions Instead of Questions

Sometimes we are asked to do something in the form of a statement, instead of a question. I call these petitions, or statements of request. Kids need to understand that petitions and questions are *almost* one and the same. I tell them that petitions are inside-out questions that need to be restated in much the same way that questions do. Petitions request that students *explain, compare, describe,* and *discuss* topics. Some question words also weave their way into petitions. For instance, we might ask someone to "Explain *how* . . ." or "Discuss *why* . . ."

At any rate, kids need experience in restating petitions, because they will indeed encounter them on tests and in life. About half the tasks on a recent grade 8 English Language Arts Assessment in New York State included petitions. Students who knew about these inside-out questions prior to that assessment were not taken aback when searching for the "question" to restate. For example, they knew that if a petition requests, "Explain how Little Red Riding Hood knew the wolf was not her grandmother," they should restate it much in the same way they would a regular question.

I also draw students' attention to the manner in which most petitions can actually be stated as questions. For instance, this petition could be reworded into the question "How did Little Red Riding Hood know the wolf was not her grandmother?"

To support lessons related to petitions, I developed the Petition Framework (Figure 7 in Chapter 3), which lists the most common petition terms. The framework also includes related information; however, we'll save the remainder for Chapter 3, where we discuss developing details.

ASSESSING CONFERRING

Assessment Type: Observation During Partner Activities

Focus Questions

- Did you use most of the words?
- Did you reread your writing? (Read it to me.)
- Does your spelling match the question's?
- Did you use a transition word? Which one?
- Did you have to substitute for any pronouns or verbs? Which ones?
- Were you restating a question or a petition?

Integrating Restating Throughout the Day

For some students, usually the younger ones, it is necessary to use several fairy tales and provide numerous restating experiences; however, most kids quickly understand how to use this first step. As a matter of fact, they enjoy transferring it into other areas of the curriculum, so that if we encounter questions in science or social studies, I might say, "Hey! Let's try to restate *these* questions as we answer them." To the students, restating quickly becomes the easy part. And that is just how we want them to feel!

Who's Using Restatements?

ACTIVITY

It's also fun to take the lead from the scientist interviewed on NPR. Students need to see how important people really do restate; it's a life skill. Therefore, we ask them to go on-line to NPR.org or PBS.org to locate interviews (especially on "Science Friday" or "Talk of the Nation") where restating is common. Students love this because it takes on the air of a scavenger hunt. It's also interesting to note how critical they can be as they notice instances where restatements were not used, but should have been.

Once some sample interviews are found, transcripts (or taped recordings for those who have Internet audio) can be collected and shared with classmates. They can also become part of next year's curriculum in restating.

Restating Old Test Questions

ACTIVITY

Another idea gathers its momentum from the formal assessment world. I offer actual (previously used) test questions for the students to restate. (Or, go to the Internet at http://www.statestandards.com, where you can find quite a variety of state standards with their assessment samples from all over the country.) If your students are like our students, they will respond, "You mean these were *real* test questions!?" And, their gestures show they are suddenly more engaged.

I save these test questions to use during a paired-partner collaboration, but I always model the first restatement for them, following the same procedure as for prior modeling. The group tends to stay more engaged, knowing that we are working with what was once "the real thing." As we proceed, I keep hoping that they are thinking, "That restating we did with fairy tales was a piece of cake—and this doesn't seem much different. Hey! I can do this!"

This simplistic Step 1 steers students right into Step 2, Constructing a Gist Answer. Step 2 may seem somewhat more intimidating at first, because it would appear that we are actually undertaking the core of the task. This is not so; in this step we seek only the general, or gist, answer, not the entire answer. But this is all explained in Chapter 2.

Construct a
Gist Answer

Learning to become literate ought to be as uncomplicated and barrier-free as possible.

(Cambourne 1988, p. 4)

Reiterating Step 1

Although we move on now to answering the question, it is important not to let restating the question take a backseat. One way to discourage this is to use the questions and restatements that were created in Step 1. Just return to those charts and extend the restatement onward into the gist answer.

Replicate the sequence of instruction as well; that is, before working with the fairy tales and their related questions, use those known-answer, personal questions. The kids need to remain steeped in simplicity, because what lies ahead is a somewhat nebulous phase of the process—one that asks students to develop a *basic*, *general*, or *gist*, answer.

What Is a General, or Gist, Answer?

What are *general*, or *gist*, answers and why do we use them? *General answers do not contain important details*. One might call them the *main idea* of the response or *the topic sentence*. They provide us only with a gist of the whole answer. We know a general answer because it makes us want to ask its author, "What do you mean?"

I've observed that most of the time when students did not incorporate enough evidence or details in their responses, it was because they had answered the test question superficially; that is, they included a couple of supportive details—a wee morsel of an answer—and then said, "That's that! I'm finished!"

In reaction to these minimally detailed answers, I decided to approach this part of the process using a minimalist perspective; that is, "If ya can't beat 'em, join 'em." And that is exactly what I did. I asked the students to develop an answer that included *no* details at all. Their answers would be only a clue to the whole answer, the gist of it. It would hint at it, but not provide detailed information. In so doing, students would create an introductory statement that was so general, it would beg for details to back it up. And, it worked!

Avenues for Teaching the Construction of Gist Answers

Unacceptable, Overly Detailed Gist Answers

One way to develop skill and understanding of this part of the process is to show students some of the *unacceptable* overly detailed answers, which might look correct, followed by *acceptable* gist answers. Let me provide an example.

The following restatements and answers sound somewhat correct, but they are not acceptable because they *initially include too much*; that is, they include too few details for a full answer, yet too many for a gist answer. So the class and I return to the pages we created earlier for our personal questions. We reread the first statement (from Chapter 1), which is followed by the ellipsis, after which I show them another chart on which I have constructed some nongist answers.

Question Prompt: What did you do last night when you got home from school?

- Last night when I got home from school I watched TV, made dinner, and went to bed.
- Last night when I got home from school I did not make supper until I had rested a bit. I was tired from such a long day.
- Last night when I got home from school I had to drive a friend to her appointment, but I made it home in time to put supper on.

We investigate the first nongist answer, discussing why it is *not* a gist answer. "This first answer is dotted with details, yet it is shallow and uninteresting," I begin. "It's too early in the paragraph to present all these details." Then I take my marker and highlight *watched TV, made dinner, went to bed.*

"No details in a gist answer," I repeat.

We go on and do the others in the same manner, but the students participate in the highlighting and the reasoning. When we finish, it is time to move into acceptable gist answers.

Acceptable Gist, or General, Answers

I tell the class that none of the previous answers was actually incorrect, but not one of them contains *all* of what is needed to defend the answer—which makes them not "correct enough." Furthermore, we have only alluded to an answer in each of them; they don't actually reveal a definite answer. Instead, they just throw a bunch of details at us.

Therefore, it's time to show students what gist answers do sound like; once they hear a few, it's amazing how quickly they catch on and fall in step with the process. So, I demonstrate how the following introductions could be good gist answers—answers that provoke *all* of the details, but contain none of them.

Question Prompt: What did you do last night when you got home from school?

- Last night when I got home from school I had fun. (What do you mean? How did you have fun?)
- Last night when I got home from school I did something exciting. (What do you mean? What did you do?)
- Last night when I got home from school I did my usual thing. (What do you mean? What is your usual thing?)

does not answer the question with any substantial information. The second applicant follows the guidelines of the Better Answer formula and comes out lookin' good and soundin' smart. Demonstrating this for preteens and teens captures their attention, and I hope will help them perform better in a real interview someday.

In Search of Gist

It's helpful to develop a running list of gist terms in statements, so students can begin categorizing what's gist and what's detail. Start them off by offering some examples related to fairy tale characters, settings, or events. For example:

- She was pretty.
- He was very brave.
- The feat was a dangerous one.
- The view was extraordinary!

After each statement, we want to ask, "What do you mean? Explain yourself." Students soon come to realize that we will need to explain, describe, or define how each term (pretty, brave, dangerous, and extraordinary) is used in the story in order to support the initial statement.

After a demonstration using known tales, students can try the same thing using characters from a book that has been read in class. Again, we demonstrate before they partner. For instance, referring to *Charlie and the Chocolate Factory*, we might state,

- Charlie is a kind boy. (What do you mean?)
- The chocolate factory was a delicious place. (What . . . mean?)
- Charlie's grandpa was generous. (What . . . mean?)

Again, students will learn far more if they construct these gist statements with a partner. Furthermore, this activity will complement and support not only this response process, but also their literature and reading curriculum.

Using Steps 1 and 2 to Review Content

It's fun and fast to present students with a whole raft of questions and their answers, then quickly let them decide which are and which are not gist answers. Again, this works best when related to the curriculum and can even serve as a source of review or study.

The students should have a large piece of tagboard on which they have printed GIST on one side and DETAILED on the other. When the teacher finishes reading a question, along with its restatement and, possibly, its gist answer, students hold up either GIST or DETAILED. For example, if the class is studying a unit on space, the teacher might ask, "Why do we need to wear special clothing in outer space?"

> *Gist answer:* We need to wear special clothing in outer space because the conditions are not like those on Earth.
> *Detailed answer:* We need to wear special clothing in outer space because it is too cold and there is no air.

After these experiences with the teacher, students enjoy creating unit questions, along with both types of answer, which can later be used for a repeat performance in class. This time it's even better, though, because the students have generated the prompts.

ASSESSING CONFERRING

Assessment Type: Test

At this point it is a good idea to help students understand that these steps should be transferring to their class tests in various subject areas. Therefore, before their next assessment, whatever that might be, remind them that their responses to performance questions should be investigated for restating and gist answers.

Focus Questions

- Did you restate using as many words from the question as possible?
- Did you construct a gist answer for that restatement?
- Does your restatement and gist answer make me want to ask, "What do you mean? Explain yourself."

Classroom Vignette Demonstrating Steps 1 and 2

Before we move on into Step 3, let's "watch" these first two steps in process through a vignette set in a grade 5 classroom. Notice how the teacher demonstrates, yet opens the process to invite students in.

Ms. Diaz finishes reading "The Three Billy Goats Gruff," and after placing the book on her desk, she lifts the top page of a large classroom chart to reveal a question. It's written on a sentence strip, but temporarily adhered to a chart, the space underneath inviting an answer.

"Who wants to be our restatement marker as we work with the first question? You'll need to underline and substitute words as the restating student restates," the teacher explains. Juan looks interested, so Ms. Diaz responds, "Juan. Want to be our marker for this first question?"

"Okay," Juan answers as he moves to the chart and picks up the black marker resting on the ledge of the chalkboard. At this point Ms. Diaz removes the strip from the chart and tapes it to the front board.

As she does this, she extends a second invitation to the group. "Okay, who will volunteer to be our scribe for writing out the dictations given during Steps 1 and 2 of the Better Answer formula? Cindi, would you like to do it, since you did not have a chance yet?"

"I hope you can read my writing," Cindi responds as she walks to the blank chart, which has had the question removed from it. Glancing back at the class questioningly, Cindi reaches for a purple marker sitting in a cup on her teacher's desk.

"It'll be fine, Cindi. Remember that this is just a rough, working draft. I'm sure we'll be able to read it," supports her teacher. However, she then adds, "But, do remember to use the question as a spelling reference to copy correctly for the restatement part, please. These are the words we know we will spell correctly because they are right there for us!" Ms. Diaz then points to the sentence and begins.

"So, the first question is 'Why did the boy continue to cry wolf when there was no wolf?' Let's restate first. Louie, would you please restate that for us?" the teacher requests, certain that Louie will competently handle her invitation.

Louie responds, "Well, uh, uh, let's see—The boy continued to . . ." and as Louie moves on with the restatement, Juan underlines and marks the original sentence in the following manner.

Why did <u>the</u> <u>boy</u> ~~continue~~ ^{continued} <u>to</u> <u>cry</u> <u>wolf</u> <u>when</u> <u>there</u> <u>was</u> <u>no</u> <u>wolf</u>?

Louie continues, ". . . cry wolf when there was no wolf because—" but he stops just after saying "because" and before he becomes involved in the answer.

At this point, Ms. Diaz steps forward. "Thanks, Louie! You stopped right in the right place." Juan goes back to his seat as Ms. Diaz turns to Cindi, who is writing Louie's restatement on the chart.

Just as Cindi is completing the last word, Ms. Diaz compliments, "Why, Cindi, that's a great job of scribing for us. Go ahead and reread it to make sure all is well, and we'll move on to the gist answer."

"Why did the boy keep crying wolf? Remember: No specifics! No details! Just a general, gist answer—one that will make us want to ask, 'What do you mean?'" Ms. Diaz prompts.

Tamar, always eager to speak up, offers, "I think it should be something about him looking for attention, or maybe trying to show off."

The teacher remains quiet, waiting for someone to respond to either Tamar or to the question. After a somewhat long, silent void the teacher suggests, "All right, let's try to work off Tamar's suggestion— unless someone else has a suggestion?" she invites one more time.

When no one responds she says, "Do you think the boy was looking for attention? Was he showing off? Joe, what do you think?"

"I think he was trying to get everyone all excited because he was bored," Joe suggests.

"So, that is similar to what Tamar is saying. How would you finish the restatement then? What would your gist answer be? What should Cindi write?" and the teacher restates the part that has already been written, "*The boy continued to cry wolf when there was no wolf because . . .*" and she smiles, raising her eyebrows at Joe to encourage his response.

Joe follows her lead with "Because . . . because he wanted to get everyone excited because he was bored."

"Okay, let's go for it!" the teacher says as she turns to Cindi again and adds, "Let's give Cindi a hand with the spelling because now she has no cues from the question." But, Cindi has confidently completed half the sentence before the teacher and the class begin their spelling support. In the end, Joe's gist answer finishes the first sentence on the chart.

Afterward the teacher asks, "What do you think, friends? Here is what we have so far: *The boy continued to cry wolf when there was no wolf because he wanted to get everyone excited because he was bored.*"

"I think there are too many becauses," interjects Ilia.

"Well, how could we fix that? How could we make it sound better?" Ms. Diaz asks.

"Could we say, 'The boy continued to cry wolf when there was no wolf because he was bored and wanted to get everyone excited?" offers Cindi, taking the lead at the front of the room.

"What do you think now, friends?" the teacher inquires. The group nods, affirming Cindi's revision.

So, Cindi dictates her own revised ending while at the same time writing it. "Looks like a one-woman band!" the teacher adds jokingly. Cindi seems pleased.

"Okay, so let's now read what Cindi has written for us, and then we can move on to restating and answering a second question," Ms. Diaz concludes. "Then, later I'd like you to work with your partner to create some questions of your own. Choose a fairy tale or fable we've read. Remember, you can use the Question Menu, too.

"Afterward, you can exchange questions with another pair of partners. Then they can use Steps 1 and 2 for your questions and you can do the same for theirs.

"Remember, though," the teacher adds, "we'll soon be moving on to Step 3, the supporting details, so I think I will keep your papers, and we can use them again when we get to Step 3—when we'll be able to add details that'll support your answers. Eventually, you will be doing this independently, just as you would have to do in a job interview or on a test. But, for now, let's work with partners."

Incorporating What We've Learned So Far

The further we venture into the formula, the easier it is to see how it connects to all subjects. As a matter of fact, by the time all five steps are completed the formula should have become enveloped in the ongoing curriculum. That means that it will be reinforced and reviewed continuously, eventually becoming second nature to the students.

By this point, it proves beneficial to encourage the use of Steps 1 and 2 during any performance assessment done in class; the fact that students have not been taught all the steps does not preclude the implementation of those they do understand. As a matter of fact, I'm always surprised just how fast they do pick up on these first two steps in the process. And, the faster they internalize Steps 1 and 2, the sooner they'll be ready to understand the importance of Step 3.

Use Details to Support Your Answer

Concreteness is now seen as necessary and unavoidable only as a stepping stone for developing abstract thinking—as a means, not an end in itself.

(Vygotsky 1978, p. 89)

More Than Just Details

Step 3 unfolds naturally out of Step 2. That is, once the gist answer is given, it tends to point the response's author directly toward the details that will support it. It is therefore a point in the process when we return to the text to search for as many details as we can find to support our response—and to thoroughly answer that begging question: "What do you mean?"

Every group that understands how to construct a restatement and a gist answer has had little trouble locating supporting details, because completing the first two steps narrows the search. Yet, finding the details is only one part of Step 3; students must also decide the order of presentation, plan how to incorporate those details into sentences that will make a coherent and cohesive paragraph, and do all this in an interesting style. To learn all this, students require a teacher who demonstrates the process, then carefully provides individual scaffolding that grows out of assessment. A considerable task!

This chapter presents methods and ideas that will lay the groundwork for raising levels of competence in this area. Chapter 4 refines and enhances what is learned in this one. Together these two chapters provide ample support for developing, in any written response, a comprehensive presentation of content.

Avenues for Teaching How to Develop Details as Evidence

The Teacher Think-Aloud Strategy

Starting Where We Left Off

Most important to this step is the teacher think-aloud strategy. This strategy calls for the teacher to make covert processes overt by sharing her mind's journey as it searches for details and then synthesizing them into a connected piece of writing. The think-aloud is an essential and strategic technique that demonstrates what's inside our heads; otherwise, how would the students know?

Let's consider what a think-aloud might include if we use it with that first personal experience question from Steps 1 and 2:

What did you do last night when you got home from school?

We have also constructed the following introduction to the details by restating and constructing a gist answer:

Last night when I got home from school I had fun.

In a think-aloud a teacher would reread the sentence and then share aloud the next steps her mind takes. She may say, "What do I mean by 'I had fun'? What kind of fun? Hm-m-m, I guess I could first list all the fun I had last night."

Entering the process in this manner leads right into drafting some detail-related notes by jotting down various "pieces" of fun that I had. As they arise in my mind, I list them and not necessarily in order. I tell the kids that I can order them and develop each into a sound sentence *after* I have my comprehensive list.

So, I stumble along my brain's path leading to a number of "fun" possibilities, some of which I keep and jot down, while others get tossed. Regardless, I continue to reveal what my brain is reasoning. In essence, what I am doing is defining what fun means to me. Once I'm pleased with my details search, I discuss the next hurdle, that is, the order I will use.

Ordering Details

We can order details in a number of ways. The following orders are the most common:

- *chronological order:* the way in which things happened in the article, essay, or story
- *order of importance:* either from most important to least important or vice versa
- *complex question order:* for questions that have several parts, we answer in the order in which they were asked

Complex question order may be a new but important consideration, because it is used on tests or when a boss asks for a report that includes several sections. In both cases we want the reader of our response to know that we did indeed include all requested parts; therefore, it makes good sense to stick to the order that was indicated in the first place. By changing that order, it may appear to a busy boss or a distracted test corrector that the responder forgot to include something. In other words, we give them the order they are expecting.

Right now, however, it makes sense for my "fun" response to be in chronological order, the way it happened last night, and I explain that decision to the group. Then, as I am numbering each detail, I think aloud why I am doing it in that manner. For example, "First, I went for a walk, so that's 1. Then, after supper I played with the baby, so that's 2." This is the first half of the detailing step. Once our notes are numbered, we have to get those details together in a connected text, which will no doubt develop into at least one paragraph.

Connecting the Pieces to Form a Cohesive Whole

"Let's see, how shall I start," I begin. Then I reread the restatement and the attached gist answer. "I'll start with number 1 first. That was this one: went for walk. How will I say that? I know, I'll say it was a nice day. Okay, so it was such a nice day that I decided to go for a walk." I then write that down right after the gist answer, which means that I have now constructed an answer that begins

> Last night when I got home from school I had fun. It was such a nice day that I decided to go for a walk.

At this point I might turn to the class and ask, "How am I doing?" Of course, they usually think the teacher is doing fine—at first.

I continue in this manner, debating various elements along the way, such as whether I should describe the walk. I decide to tell a little bit about it, because what happened along the way was what made the walk fun. It backs up my gist. I must stick to those experiences that were fun, experiences that provide evidence for my gist. I keep reviewing this strategy.

Other Anchors

Because these introductory demonstration lessons always feed off read-alouds, the students will not have a text in front of them. In instances where they do, however, they may certainly use underlining and highlighting to reveal more details. A demonstration transparency also allows for such marking during a common viewing experience. Now we have come to the point in the process when we can leave those personal questions behind and use only familiar tales for the development of our anchor experiences.

Chapter 4 provides another example of a think-aloud. It is used with a write-aloud to illustrate how Steps 3 and 4 look in a classroom, and it will provide yet another perspective for this technique. The remainder of this chapter includes ideas and activities to support teaching students how to develop details. One of the most supportive structures and my favorite is the Answer Sandwich. It works nicely in tandem with the think-aloud. Furthermore, through this concrete structure we can easily show kids how to end a response.

The Answer Sandwich: A Concrete Writing Framework

Teachers find the Answer Sandwich a very effective tool—a kind of fool-proof method that, for the struggling response writer, makes an abstract process more concrete. Let me share the manner in which I introduce it and why it helps writers focus on details that support the answer.

With students who have been steeped in Steps 1 and 2, I display a transparency of the Answer Sandwich (Figure 1). The form can also be transferred onto a chart that has been laminated with plastic, so it can be reused.

Figure 1

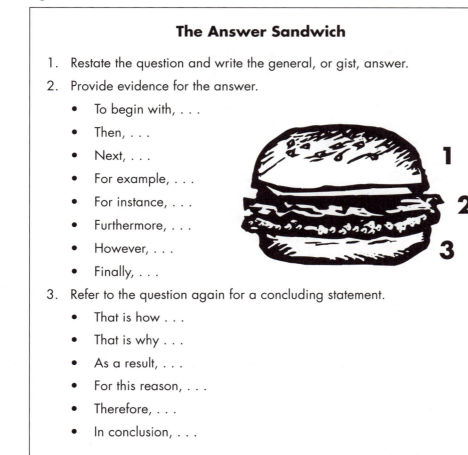

The Answer Sandwich

1. Restate the question and write the general, or gist, answer.
2. Provide evidence for the answer.
    *   To begin with, . . .
    *   Then, . . .
    *   Next, . . .
    *   For example, . . .
    *   For instance, . . .
    *   Furthermore, . . .
    *   However, . . .
    *   Finally, . . .
3. Refer to the question again for a concluding statement.
    *   That is how . . .
    *   That is why . . .
    *   As a result, . . .
    *   For this reason, . . .
    *   Therefore, . . .
    *   In conclusion, . . .

Ordering the Sandwich Layers

I first discuss the three parts of the sandwich, suggesting to the group that the top bun (layer 1) and the bottom bun (layer 3) are very similar—just like a real sandwich! The middle section (layer 2) has several layers (details), also just like a real sandwich.

Another similar quality relates to this graphic's ordered layers; that is, in a real sandwich, peanut butter goes on before jelly. The Answer Sandwich also has a particular order, which follows one of the sequences discussed at the beginning of this chapter.

Using Transitions to Glue Sentences Together

Furthermore, a number of transition terms are related to the sandwich's order; when used appropriately, they can make the writer look good and sound smart. Several common transitions are on the Answer Sandwich display chart; however, a wide variety of these terms can be used as connectors that glue the sentences of a paragraph together. These will be internalized and incorporated more readily into student writing if the teacher models their use during the demonstration lessons, and even more so when students are scaffolded toward their use in context during writing conferences. Developing charts of the following options will provide a ready reference for students and the teacher alike.

Transitions That Order

Chronological Order

first	finally
next	at last
second	near the bottom
at the top	the following
to begin with	afterward
then	heretofore
additionally	

Order of Importance

most/least important
most serious
most/least significant
a major/minor factor

Order of Effect or Relatedness

as a result
on the other hand
in connection
related to this
unrelated to this

Transitions with Various Purposes

Transitions That Show Cause

because	as a result
for this reason	so
therefore	consequently

Transitions That Show Contrast

however	whereas
on the other hand	while
but	moreover
yet	despite this

Transitions That Show Comparison

similarly	and
like	again
in like manner	much the same as
also	furthermore
likewise	

Transitions That Show Examples

for instance	to illustrate
for example	that is

The Sandwich: Part 1

To model use of the framework that the Answer Sandwich offers, I use a question from a familiar fairy tale and move through a think-aloud to place my responses on a double-entry, two-column chart, the Answer Organizer (Figure 2), created for this purpose. The Answer Organizer has

Figure 2

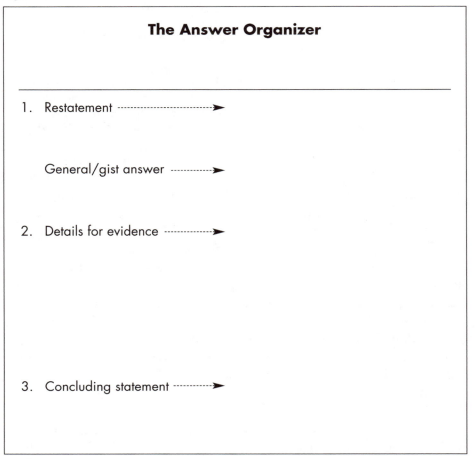

Figure 3

The Answer Organizer

Question: How did Little Red Riding Hood know that the character in the bed was not her grandmother?

1.   Restatement ·························➤   Little Red Riding Hood knew that the character in the bed was not her grandmother

    General/gist answer ············➤   because that character did not look or sound like her grandmother.

2.   Details for evidence ···········➤   She noticed that his voice was gruff, not like her grandmother's voice. Also, that character in the bed had very large eyes, unlike her grandmother's. But most important, what she noticed were his teeth. They were huge!

3.   Concluding statement ··········➤   That is how Little Red Riding Hood knew that character was not her grandmother, and it's a good thing she noticed!

---

the sandwich's parts listed on the left and space to write on the right. Figures 3 and 4 support the early steps into this process because sections for each part in the organizer are completed. (Their related stories can be found in the appendixes.) I often use one of them as my model.

Again working from a familiar tale, I invite students into Step 1 by displaying the related question prompt. First, I call for the restating part, scribing one dyad's words in the right-hand column next to "1. Restatement" (from Part 1 of the Answer Sandwich), as shown in Figures 2 and 3. After allowing time for Step 2, I call for a gist answer, which is then scribed next to "General/Gist Answer" (also from Part 1 of the Answer Sandwich). The top bun is the easy part.

The Sandwich: Part 2

Now we are ready to search for details for evidence (for Part 2 of the sandwich). I suggest that partners do as I did; that is, they should move away

Figure 4

The Answer Organizer

Question: Why were the three bears so upset when they got home from their walk?

---

1. Restatement ┄┄┄┄┄┄┄┄┄┄┄▶ The three bears were upset when they got home because

   General/gist answer ┄┄┄┄┄┄▶ their house was not like they left it.

2. Details for evidence ┄┄┄┄┄▶ To begin with, the bears noticed that someone had been eating their porridge. Next they discovered that someone had broken baby bear's chair. Furthermore, their beds were messed up. Most important, however, was that there was a little girl IN one of the beds!

3. Concluding statement ┄┄┄┄▶ As a result of all that confusion the three bears were very upset.

---

from the double-column chart and onto a piece of scrap paper, where they can jot down the details to support a gist answer. After they have time to gather some details, I invite the partners to offer possibilities, which I scribe onto a large chart in no particular order.

Then, together we organize the scribed notes. First we decide what order will make sense to best support our gist answer. Next, we select the place each detail will hold, numbering them 1, 2, 3, and so on. Some we decide not to use. Consequently, the list gets pared to only the most essential details, as we continually ask, "Do I really need this to support the gist answer?"

After we have numbered the details, we develop each into a sentence, just as we did before. At this time I introduce and strongly encourage the use of transitions to connect sentence pieces into a whole context. Transitions offer such obvious glue to a piece that each becomes a small anchor for lookin' good and soundin' smart. Once students begin to use these, their writing takes on a new level of maturity—and the best part is, they know it!

All of this is done collaboratively. The whole class offers suggestions, and throughout we keep rereading our writing to make sure it makes sense. Sometimes we even change our minds and cross things out. Eventually, we get to the point where we have considered all the supportive details, and chosen which to include. Then we're ready to develop an ending for our piece of writing—just as I did in the model I presented beforehand.

The Sandwich: Part 3

With the middle of the sandwich complete, we move on to the bottom bun, the concluding statement. When I introduce this structure to students I encourage them to simply create a kind of restatement of the introduction (or top bun). They can begin with "That is why . . ." or "That is how . . . ," just as I did in the Answer Organizer for "Little Red Riding Hood": "That is how Little Red Riding Hood knew that character was not her grandmother."

Alongside the Concluding Statement section of the organizer and after partners have had a chance to collaborate, I call for one dyad to dictate its concluding statement, which I then scribe in its proper location on the chart. In so doing, we offer a sense of finality to the piece.

A Touch of Voice

Once students gain confidence and competence, I scaffold them toward incorporating more voice into this concluding section. I suggest that they can create the following types of connection in the bottom bun:

- a personal connection
- a world connection
- a text connection
- a connection to the author's craft

I believe that it is important to save such connections for the very end of a test response or a serious report to an employer. That is not to say, however, that on all essays voice should be squeezed into the last lines. There are multiple essay types where voice is indeed woven in and out and about, for instance, those we hear daily on National Public Radio. However, when we encourage young students to try to weave voice into the middle of their answers, they often get carried away and go off on a tangent. Saving personal reflections, opinions, and connections for the end leaves the reader with a taste of voice, yet limits the writer on the amount. It also keeps him from tainting his answer, because it has already been presented.

A whole book could be written related to the kinds of connections that can be made within an essay response. It is not always easy to teach these connections to students, so I suggest lots of think-alouds. Harvey and Goudvis (2000) provide wonderful background for instructional strategies related to this connections process.

Working our way through the Answer Sandwich often takes more than one lesson, that is, more than one day. Yet, it is worth the time spent because the students feel secure with its framework and tend to rely on it during these early stages in the process. Some will probably always rely on it to help them get through an essay or a response.

Exact Facts or Cool and Creative Fiction?

Usually at least one student falls into creative writing in the midst of a test response; that is, Manuel may compose a beautiful essay response and, just as he is trying to conclude the piece, he might slip into fantasy and concoct a completely new ending for the text he read. Instead of saying a character should've, would've, could've, he says the character actually did it! Not "Goldilocks *should* never go back into that house again," but rather, "Goldilocks never went back into that house again." The former may be a somewhat clever ending; the latter is just plain inappropriate.

Fourth grader Sean recently meandered off the story line during a lesson. I had read the fable of the "Bear and the Bees" to the group, and he had answered the question quite nicely, adhering to specific details from the story. But then, at the very end of his little essay response, he deviated. Instead of saying what Bear could have done or what might happen the next time Bear encountered a similar situation, he began telling what Bear did next—when there was no next! Instead of constructing a conclusion, Sean constructed a whole new ending.

Other students take similar wrong turns in their responses. They add small fabrications here and there because they think it is clever or makes their writing more interesting. Just today Maria told us that the bear "grabbed the log with his teeth, showed his claws, and growled." The bear did the first two things, but Maria was on a roll, so she just extended it a bit with a small embellishment. To a child's way of thinking, this makes the response even better, but I explain to them that it is not appropriate for this kind of task. Nor is it appropriate for many real-world tasks.

The fine lines existing in these situations make clarifying difficult. I found that it helps to explain that some adult tasks require us to be "cool and creative," and other tasks call for us to present the "exact facts." For example, a landscaper who runs into a problem may need a worker who has some cool and creative ideas she could commit to print, but a newspaper reporter stationed in a war zone would be expected to report only the facts. Kids understand the lines of demarcation here. Thus, I suggest that they act much like news reporters when they are taking a performance assessment. That is, they should not be cool and creative unless the task does indeed ask them to write creatively. Otherwise, they should act like a reporter and stick to exact facts.

Fact or Fiction?

To help students more fully understand what is appropriate to include in an essay response, I construct a T-chart. I label the left side "Exact Facts" and the right side "Cool and Creative," and begin the lesson by reading aloud a short story or tale such as "Goldilocks and the Three Bears." When I finish I give each student a copy of the story. However, I also pass out index cards, on some of which I have written a story-related fact, while others contain a fictional sentence or phrase.

Each student then takes a turn to come and place his or her card under the heading best suited. But, as the student does this he or she knows to be prepared to answer the question: Why do you think your card belongs in that column? Some examples follow.

For instance, if the story was "Goldilocks and the Three Bears" (the version in the appendix), some facts may be

- Goldilocks's mother was often afraid. ("a fearful sort")
- Goldilocks could tell Mama Bear's porridge was hot, so she passed it up. ("noticed steam rising . . . thus circumvented it")
- Papa Bear comforted his daughter when she was upset. ("to console her . . . picked her up . . . hugged her")

Although these statements are facts from the story, I did not state them in exactly the same manner that the story did. For that reason, to prove their point students need to return to the story's evidence for their choice of card placement.

It is easy to see how kids might confuse reworded statements with creative deviations from the facts. The following examples could be placed in the cool and creative column:

- The police are going to arrest Goldilocks for breaking and entering.
- Goldilocks's mother does not care about her, or she would not allow her child to roam the woods alone.
- The bears spent a lot of time cleaning up after Goldilocks.

This last example is a very common type, because it is actually a post-story prediction. Students who have been appropriately encouraged to predict "what happens next" throughout primary-grade reading lessons tend to use that path when it is inappropriate.

Furthermore, although very careful consideration should be given to discouraging use of cool and creative statements on performance assessments, it's a good idea to ask students to decide what might be an occasion when those cool and creative responses would be appropriate. We *do* want students to be cool and creative; we just don't want them to misuse such writing on exact-fact tests.

"The Stranger" Technique

A Lack of Audience Consideration

As writers crawl into the details of a piece, they often forget their audience, and they write as though the reader already possesses background information. At this point I invite "the Stranger" into the classroom. This technique was developed out of an immediate need when I was conferring with students in Barb McKay's fourth grade. Barb had been working with the Better Answer formula and had asked me to come in and help "grease the wheels" where it was needed.

I decided to start with individual conferences, the most effective technique for scaffolding students. During those conferences I noticed a kind of pattern among the group—a pattern I had seen the previous year when working with fifth-grade students. That is, they tended to write as if the reader would already know much of the information—information that was consequently omitted.

Such lack of awareness of audience causes students to overdose on pronouns (*She* left *her* when *her* mother . . .), use lone referents (They didn't go there because of *what happened*), and omit important evidence that could support their answers. Unfortunately, this minimalist approach leaves the reader of such a response clueless. This neglect to consider an audience was exactly what I was observing in those fourth-grade responses, and I struggled to bring this problem into the students' awareness.

Enter the Stranger

Gropingly, I asked one fourth grader with whom I was working, "Sonya, what if the principal, or some stranger, came down the hall and read this? Think about it. What would that stranger want to know if he read only your answer?" I then got up, walked down the hall a few feet, and returned personifying "the Stranger."

"Oh, hi, little girl. I'm from Channel 4 and we are visiting your school today to see what the students are doing," I pretended. "What's this you're doing? Is it okay if I read over your shoulder?"

"Sure," laughed Sonya, playing along.

So I began to read over her shoulder, "In the story 'The Lion and the Mouse' the mouse proved the lion was wrong because he—hm-m, he? he? Does Sonya mean the mouse?" I subvocalized loudly enough so Sonya could hear my covert thinking. "Or he, the lion? . . . because he got him out from being caught. Hm-m, who got whom out? And what was he caught in? What does she mean?"

After my Stranger act, Sonya responded, "Oh, I get it. I have to explain it more!"

"Exactly. And replace all those pronouns with nouns, because the Channel 4 anchorwoman does not know who the hes and shes are," I suggested. "Just keep thinking that the Stranger is standing over your shoulder observing your response. What would he want to know? What would bother him and make him go, 'Huh? What does she mean?'"

Later, I shared with Sonya's teacher what I had done with Sonya, as well as several others who also needed the Stranger looking over their shoulders. Barb, their teacher, thought it sounded like a good idea and said she would continue to use it. We also discussed how it would be helpful if, the next time her class answered some questions, the other fourth-grade group could read them and act as the Strangers.

A couple of weeks later Barb stopped me in the hall and exclaimed, "The Stranger is working wonders in our room! I wish he had visited in September!"

We also came to realize that if the Stranger is unable, simply by reading the answer, to infer the question that was being asked, then the answer is not complete. In other words, every answer should be able to stand alone and make sense without its question. It should be a little stand-alone essay. This is important for students to understand.

Lots of Work for the Stranger

Since that time I have shared the Stranger with many other teachers and have taken him or her to a variety of other classrooms from grades 3 through 8. That Stranger works wonders every time! The teachers and I have even put on coats and hats and disguised our voices to add more realism. In School 45 in Buffalo the curriculum director, Mary Ann Hopfer, asked the art teacher to make "Stranger" posters with a few writers' guidelines for all grades 3 through 8 classrooms! They now hang as ready reminders to write for an audience, one of whom might be the Stranger.

I only wish the Stranger had visited the reading classes I taught at the university, because my college students often displayed some of the same shortcomings in their writing. Even in reviewing journal articles for two professional organizations, I continually write in the margins, asking the author the same questions that the Stranger would ask. Obviously, the

Stranger is going to have a very big job ahead of him, so it's best to invite him in asap!

The Better Answer Scale

Another important aspect of Step 3 is the introduction of the Better Answer scale (Figure 5), the assessment tool that helps students understand specifically where they need to focus the greatest amount of their energy. It also shows the teacher where to concentrate instruction for any given student, as well as for directed group lessons.

Many teachers ask, "Why did you use a three-point scale?" My answer: "To keep it simple." Today's students and teachers are inundated with rubrics for every subject, some of which are very complex. Such rubrics may be entirely necessary; however, for our purpose here, this three-point scale works like a charm. Students know that they are either doing it, almost doing it, or minimally doing it. Simple! Plus, teachers aren't sitting around deliberating over all the descriptors in a six-point scale.

For students who offer no evidence in one of the answer attributes (for instance, they do not restate the question at all), I simply leave that area blank on their scale. In this way, if they revise their answer, I can then fill in a score. Teachers who prefer a four-point scale can simply extend the scoring levels to include a 0, the score for students who demonstrate no evidence in a given area.

Figure 5

The Better Answer Scale

Name _____ Date _____

	Minimally 1	Partially 2	Completely 3
Restates question in the answer	_____	_____	_____
Develops a gist answer	_____	_____	_____
Uses details from text to support the answer	_____	_____	_____
Develops conclusion	_____	_____	_____
Stays on topic	_____	_____	_____
Writes very neatly	_____	_____	_____
Uses proper conventions	_____	_____	_____

It's easy to see that the first four areas on the Better Answer scale replicate Steps 1, 2, and 3 in the Better Answer formula, that is, all of those we have heretofore discussed. Stay on the Topic is actually an extension and a refinement of Uses Details from Text to Support the Answer and therefore also deals with the content of the writing.

However, Step 5 in the formula, Use Proper Conventions, is broken down, extracting handwriting as an entity unto itself. Both handwriting and conventions concern the cosmetics and mechanics of the piece. This step asks, Can we easily read what has been written here?

I like the way Peter Elbow (1981) sculpts this issue. He says, "When the glass is fogged up, we look at the glass. The glass is all we see. As soon as it gets unfogged we ignore it and see through it to the scene outside" (p. 94). Kids need to understand this. They need to know why it is important to write neatly, and why they must place a priority on bringing the conventions to an optimal level.

Interestingly, we discover that our students are better handwriters than we might have believed, as becomes evident each time I introduce the Better Answer scale to a group of students. The first time I introduce this rubric to a class, I explain, "Every time you do a brief, extended, or essay response in any subject, we will be attaching this rubric to your work so that you can keep track of your progress in developing an answer."

I then suggest that it would be helpful for them to circle the area that will be their focus for that particular task that day. I say, "Each time we use this rubric, I would like you to focus on one part in particular, so that on any given paper your circled area will most likely end up being an area where you show improvement. Choose any of the six this first time, but pick one in which you truly believe you will be able to show a quality performance and, hopefully, receive a 3."

Students always choose the same part as their first focus. Can you guess which one? If you said handwriting, you are correct. You see, kids know that they have control over their handwriting, even though they do not always use that control. Nor, for that matter, do we ourselves always use it. However, adults do spiff up handwriting when it counts—when it's important to look good. And we need to confess this to our students.

Once they circle "Handwriting" as their focus, looking for an optimal score in that area, they often get it. The second area for their choice of focus is usually "Restates the question," because it, too, is one over which they quickly have considerable command. Thus, in a very short time, they're able to receive a top score in two areas—even the struggling students can! This makes everyone feel good and look smart.

When papers do obtain a quality appearance, I make sure that I draw that to the students' attention, and I usually try to connect it to the real world. I hold up Joe's paper and say, "Wow! If Joe handed this in as a job application and I were his boss, I would really look at him in a positive way. See how neat his paper is! That predicts for me that the rest of his work will also be neat and well done. And, he even indented! That *really* makes you look smart!" These are very easy ways for students to look good, which then gives them the impetus to sound smart.

The grade 4 teachers at School 45 in Buffalo have been using the Better Answer scale throughout the curriculum. They say it helps students understand how these steps can support them when they construct written responses anywhere. It is also somewhat of a relief for students to know that what they learn in language arts can also be conveniently used in social studies, science, and other content areas—as well as in real life.

Thick and Thin Questions

In Chapter 1 a large variety of questions and petitions were presented (see Figures 6 and 7). As students continually use these to construct their own questions and petitions, they begin to understand that certain questions quite often predict a particular kind of response. We need students to know the predictable kinds of responses that certain questions provoke. This means it would be helpful if they understood the codependency between questions and their answers.

It's beneficial to point out the qualities of particular question terms and their relation to details. That is, some question terms evoke a more in-depth, rich response, and others call for a brief, surface response. For instance, *why, how,* and *might* questions generally call for some in-depth searching and connecting. They tend to evoke deep, rich responses that require more paper space to answer. Harvey and Goudvis (2000) call these "thick" responses. Whereas, questions beginning with *who, where,* and *when* often call for less lengthy, easily located, surface details. The two authors call these "thin" responses. I take the concept a step further by calling the questions themselves thick and thin. In other words, *who* usually elicits a brief response and would therefore be called a *thin question*.

Furthermore, thin questions are frequently literal and evoke surface-structure answers that can usually be located right there in the observable text. They can also easily be evidenced as correct or incorrect: When? On December 12, 1942. Where? In Northern Italy. I tell the kids this so they won't spend an inordinate amount of time collecting a bushel of details to answer a thin question, especially when thick questions lie in wait. I know they fall prey to this because I have been a corrector of the state perform-ance assessments on which many students spend too much time on thin questions and then pay for it later when they lack the time to answer a thick one. We need to help them understand the questions whose

Figure 6

Better Questions Menu

	Time: Past	Present	Prediction	Character	Setting	Events	Problem-Solution	Cause-Effect	Time Order	Compare Contrast	Description	Evaluation
Who is												
Who was												
Who can												
Who does												
Who did												
Who will												
Who might												
Who should												
Who could												
Who had												
Where is												
Where was												
Where can												
Where does												
Where did												
Where will												
Where might												
Where should												
Where could												
Where had												
When is												
When was												
When can												
When does												
When did												
When will												
When might												
When should												
When could												
When had												
Why is												
Why was												

Why can	Why does	Why did	Why will	Why might	Why should	Why could	Why had	What is	What was	What can	What does	What did	What will	What might	What should	What could	What had	How is	How was	How can	How does	How did	How will	How might	How should	How could	How had	Which is	Which was	Which can	Which does	Which did	Which will	Which might	Which should	Which could	Which had

Figure 7

The Petition Framework

Key Petition Terms	Meaning	Framework	Examples
Analyze (common with why and how)	Separate into its parts.	An ordered list framework containing parts or steps	Analyze the personality of the main character.
Compare	Examine, noting similarities and differences.	Venn diagram to show differences of each with likeness in the center	Compare two ways of doing something.
Contrast	Examine, noting the differences only.	T-chart (two columns below a heading) to contrast left to right	Contrast two or more approaches.
Define	State a precise meaning or the basic qualities of something.	An ordered list or outline framework	Define the term used.
Discuss (common with why and how)	Present background information with supporting or descriptive details.	T-chart with important factors on left, details on right	Discuss the minor events leading to a major event.
Describe (common with why and how)	Convey an idea, qualities, or background information.	Semantic web: subject in middle, surrounded by numbered qualities	Describe a person, place, thing, or event.
Evaluate	Place judgment, but support using details.	T-chart listing pros next to cons	Evaluate the actions, behaviors, or decisions of individuals or groups.
Explain (common with how and why)	Make clear or offer reason.	T-chart listing facts and supportive details	Explain an action or how/why something happened.
Give/provide	Offer facts related to topic.	T-chart using facts and supportive details	Give several reasons, examples, possibilities, alternatives.
Review	Examine major elements again, sometimes using a critical perspective.	Outline or list framework	Review paths followed, steps taken, important events.
Tell (common with how and why)	Offer facts related to topic.	T-chart using facts and supportive details	Give several reasons, examples, possibilities, alternatives.
Use	Do the task in a specific manner.	Outline or list framework	Use details or information to support.
Write	Usually use as a prompt for a specific task.	Outline or list framework	Write: about; telling; explaining; describing.

responses will require their greatest efforts, so they do not misplace time and energy on thin questions.

On the other hand, thick questions, such as *why* and *how*, are of a different nature, provoking interesting, exciting, and sometimes debatable answers. Consequently, they involve more explanation, more details. They call to our deep structure requiring us to crawl down between the lines, to revisit prior text and background knowledge, to make subtle connections between what the text is saying and what our experiences suggest. Such details may require a grand search, and as a consequence, thick questions require far more time to answer.

It therefore makes sense to teach students these differences. Invite them to investigate by trying the questions on for size. Support them in question development by providing opportunities to do so. Only by exploring questions and petitions as a whole will they come to understand the predictable differences in their parts.

In Search of Thick and Thin

ACTIVITY

A simple sorting activity can help students begin to distinguish the depth of questions and expected answers. In this activity we provide partners with a sheet of questions from the Question Menu, which they cut apart, then place each question under the related heading: Thick or Thin.

Obviously, this provokes some conversation and maybe even some debates. But this is what we want. We want kids comparing thick and thin questions, understanding question commonalities and differences, and climbing into the depths of a culture of inquiry. This activity can serve only as the tip of the iceberg.

Why is this important? It's important because developing deep, rich answers for the thick questions is a school assessment skill, but it is also a real-life career skill. When the supervisor asks a thick question like "Why are sales down?" it's probably not wise to answer with a thin response such as "People are not buying." That supervisor, no doubt, wants to know every single detail related to why sales are down, so that the company can do something about it. "People are not buying" is an answer, but it is a gist, or general, answer. It is a surface-structure answer. The boss wants the details to back it up, just as we discussed in building the Answer Sandwich.

Considering Question Attributes

ACTIVITY

After students have a background in thick and thin questions, we can move on to other question categories—categories that will help them capably spot related details. Most adults realize that when a question begins with *who*, its answer probably involves a person or people. Likewise, *when* relates to time and *where* to place. As students come to understand such relationships, they become more capable of skimming and scanning material for specific information. The Better Question Menu (Figure 6) lists some types of connections along the top horizontal axis.

Struggling readers tend to use the same strategy for every question; that is, they start at the beginning of the piece and read straight through until they come to the answer. These students need lots of experience matching *who* questions with people and *where* questions with places.

The obvious strategy for scaffolding students in this area may appear to be to have them locate the in-text answers for each specific question type, help them skim for specific details, and show them how to search for the capital letters related to important places and people. All that is well and good, and it does help, but I suggest that we turn the ownership around; that is, let the students develop the related questions from their content material. They will internalize the process when they must search for the context, the details, in order to compose the question—just as we teachers do when we construct their tests.

This activity can serve as a review or reinforcement for necessary content concepts, as well as supporting those question-answer codependent relationships that were mentioned previously. To begin, invite partners to develop one question (related to a current unit of study) for each of the following categories:

time
place
people
past
present
future

Then, to satisfy those who would rather see the students answer the questions, invite each dyad to trade their questions with another pair of students. Both pairs will be expected to use the Better Answer formula to respond to some of the questions. Afterward, each pair can pass its answers back to the questions' authors, instead of the teacher. The creators of the questions can easily correct the answers since they developed the questions out of the answers in the first place. In this kind of back-and-forth activity the codependency of questions and answers becomes evident. Furthermore, it makes an interesting way to study content.

Assessment Type: The Better Answer Scale

Students are now ready to make steady use of this scale across the curriculum. That is, if the class is having a health test on which one part asks that they explain how the stomach digests food, we expect them to transfer the Better Answer protocol to that performance task. To emphasize this across-the-day use, we usually staple a (reduced, quarter-page) Better Answer scale to the corner of each response page beforehand. In that way, it becomes a visible nudge for constructing a sound answer. The mark they receive on the scale is usually logged as a language arts score.

Focus Questions

Questions from the answer scale drive both the assessment and the conferring sessions. Afterward, when meeting with individual students, we often work from their corrected papers (with the scale attached). We focus on positive points first, and then end the conference with one scale area that needs improvement, as well as a possible strategy to bring this about.

End-of-Unit Petitions

The Petition Framework (Figure 7) chart helps structure thinking so that students understand how particular petitions lead quite naturally to related answer avenues. Accordingly, when presented with a petition asking that they analyze, students have a head start, knowing that they can begin with the framework of a list that is probably going to contain parts or steps. Consequently, their search for details is narrowed to a search for steps or a list of people, places, or events. Other areas on the framework also narrow their details search.

How can we have students internalize all the facets of the Petition Framework? There are myriad ways, but let me provide one activity that works well and complements the end of any unit of study. First, select a number of areas from that unit that are necessary for its understanding. Very often these can simply be lifted from core documents of state standards (www.statestandards.com). Then present these important areas to the students.

For instance, if the students are studying the Revolutionary War, certain concepts and understandings will be identified as core, or most important. In this case, it might be the manner in which the war began, those who fought in the war, the major battles, the reasons for the war, and so on. Because it is the end of the unit, students should possess some background in these areas; therefore, I ask partners to work with those areas to develop suitable petitions for each. This means they will take the content to the petition, search for the best match, and then develop a petition. As partners collaborate using the Petition Framework, they begin to internalize its contents.

Furthermore, their collection of petitions makes a fine resource for the actual unit assessment. And, why not use the students' own questions!

We Aren't There Yet!

It would seem that once we have students to this point in the answer journey, the content is complete; they have developed a whole answer. Unfortunately, this is not usually the case. Rather, it is here that we often start to notice a different kind of problem. This is a time when students are prone to overelaborate and to get off-topic, particularly when their confidence builds. How do we tell a student he has included too much when he is the same student who, before the Better Answer formula, wrote one sentence? How do students learn what is too much and what is not enough? And how do we show our new writing zealots how to stay on topic? Read on.

Stay on the Topic

Conferring well with students requires that I have a vision of what I hope for them as writers. Just as listening up close has everything to do with how to confer, stepping back to see the big picture is equally important.

(Hindley 1996, p. 42)

Overflowing Cups of Confidence

Just when it appears that students are able to appropriately construct the content of a response, a new problem arises. For once they learn to develop a detailed answer, they have trouble staying on the topic. Therefore, Chapter 4 investigates this new but common obstacle and offers some supportive activities. Interestingly, part of the reason that their detailed evidence metamorphoses into a new stage of difficulties is that by the time students work their way through Step 3, their cup of confidence is overflowing—and so is their writing.

Most students move easily through restating the question and constructing an answer. With regular teacher modeling, they also learn where and how to gather the details to support their answers, lengthening and strengthening their piece of writing. This is the first time some students have performed this way in the written world, and they are proud that they have "filled the page." This bolsters the writer's ego. Working off this somewhat inflated ego, they get carried away with the writing and tell every single thing that comes to mind. Sometimes they copy every word in the text! At other times they make several connections to their own experiences, deviating from a mandated focus on textual evidence. From their perspective, more is better. So they write and they write and they write.

This is one of the toughest times for me, as their teacher, because they are feeling so good about what they are doing. Some of these kids are learning disabled or have been consistent reading students, and they joyously call me over to exclaim, "Hey, look! I filled the whole page!" I find it difficult to tell them that they must now eliminate some of those precious words. This is not relevant only for struggling students and beginning writers; this is a problem for all writers. We hate to eliminate our words—our "little darlings," Stephen King (2000) calls them. But even he says we must do this "even when it breaks your egocentric little scribbler's heart." King follows a "Rewrite Formula" a reviewer once gave him: "2nd Draft = 1st Draft − 10%" (p. 222). Somehow it is comforting to know that even the likes of Stephen King have trouble staying on the topic.

Avenues for Teaching Students How to Stay On Topic

Leave It in or Leave It Out?

Revision at this point in the process usually means cutting, substituting, and (infrequently) extending. Mostly it means cutting. To enter such an elimination of words with grace and finesse, I model . . . and model . . . and model, hoping that what students observe will be contagious. It usually is not. However, the modeling still serves as the ground into which I can help them plant their own seeds. In other words, as I chat with them about their writing, I can anchor them back into my modeled piece and what I did, while making an analogy to theirs and what they might want to do. Often I leave my modeled pieces posted, for ready reference. However, be forewarned, students still hate to eliminate any part of their writing. Yet they, like King (2000), eventually learn that "the effect of judicious cutting is immediate and often amazing" (p. 222). I just keep inviting them to join the old King-Cole Cutting Club.

Numbering every possible detail in its order of importance, from most to least, forces students to discern important from less important information. We might suggest that they keep only the essential details, the ones with the lowest numbers, while eliminating those assigned the highest numbers. Yet, there are other ways to assist students in this facet of the process.

Highlighting Important Details

One of the six important comprehension strategies (see Harvey and Goudvis 2000) involves discerning important from unimportant details. Many students think everything they read is important. They therefore assume that everything must be in their answer.

In working with struggling readers, who generally maintain this perspective, I have found that modeling important details using a highlighter or a yellow crayon helps. I also use a pencil sometimes to leave tracks in the margins for later reference. Whatever way you choose, all those tracks (highlighted or penciled) are important. They become the keys to the answer kingdom. But, we need to show kids how this process works.

I first explain the purpose of the task. For instance, it might be to find out why the *Titanic* sank (I always use something really interesting when modeling). I would begin by reading aloud, stopping here and there to think aloud, highlight, and jot in the margins. When I think something is really important, I put exclamation marks or sunbeams shooting out from it. Obviously, this works best when I use a transparency and the kids use consumable materials. With nonconsumables, use Post-its.

Afterward, I go back and explain my reasoning in dubbing much of the information as *unimportant*. For instance, I might say, "If I am searching for reasons why the *Titanic* sank, it would not seem to matter what color the ship was, nor how some people didn't use the rescue boats properly, nor the number of children on board. That information may have been important in answering other questions, but it does not seem important when I am searching for why the ship sank."

Uncovering the unimportant is an essential piece of this step, because students need to hear us say the words, "This is not important because . . ." They need validation that indeed there are parts of text that have absolutely nothing to do with the question asked.

Even so, "Leave it in?" or "Leave it out?" will continue to plague many students. I find the two best ways to help struggling students discern important from unimportant ideas are modeling unplanned, authentic writing and through mindful scaffolding during individual conferences. I can almost guarantee success using these two instructional avenues.

Modeling Unplanned, Authentic Writing

There is an enormous difference between a planned modeling lesson and an unplanned one. Most often teachers are told to plan, plan, plan, if they want great lessons. However, when we plan a modeling lesson for writing, everything turns out a bit too neat and clean and perfect. Writing is not neat and clean and perfect. Writing is usually messy and disorganized, and first efforts are sometimes pretty shabby. As a matter of fact, teachers who have seen my rough-draft messes have asked me if they could have the draft copied to use as an example in their classes.

Students need to observe a writer's messes. Real ones! They also need to see the convoluted manner in which we think our way through constructing an answer. They need to observe how we go back and forth, back and forth, between the text and the writing. Most of all they need to hear how our minds speak to us as we do this. The best way to demonstrate this is through a think-aloud/write-aloud *unplanned* experience.

Think-Alouds and Write-Alouds

Think-alouds and write-alouds (TAWAs) interpret covert thinking into overt processes that can occur when constructing a written piece. They help students observe the spontaneous and myriad thoughts that come while creating or composing.

Just as in previous demonstrations, I use fairy tales and fables for TAWAs. These familiar tales not only help the students to feel more comfortable, they also support me, their teacher, during those first TAWA lessons, which, because they are spontaneous, can be a bit intimidating. After the first few, however, they are actually fun and end up weaving their way into many periods of my teaching. Furthermore, the kids love them because they can observe their instructor in a state of semiconfusion—a time when their teacher does *not* know all the answers. Even adults request, "Don't just tell me, show me." Certainly, TAWAs are important for many reasons.

Classroom Vignette Demonstration for Steps 3 and 4

Perhaps the best way to illustrate this is through another classroom vignette. This TAWA is grounded in the fairy tale "The Three Little Pigs."

"Would all of you find a seat, because I have something I want to show you?" Ms. Hildreth announces to her class. As the students settle into their usual spots, their teacher pulls a large blank chart into place in front of them. Scattered about the room, the seventh graders soon grow more still and quiet, ready to begin.

The teacher goes on, "Our class is getting good at answering essay questions, but we can do better than good. Terrific answers take a lot of thinking. We're doing fine, but we can always strive to do better. So, today I'm going to show you something that I bet you'll enjoy."

At this point, she notices a couple of students who look at each other and then roll their eyes, so Ms. Hildreth responds, "Seriously! You'll enjoy it mainly because it'll show you that teachers also struggle in finding the right answer. We, just like you, friends, have to think about the question and how it relates to parts of the story—parts that could be included in the answer. I had to write essays in that graduate class I took last semester. Ever see a teacher struggle? Just watch."

Having now gained everyone's attention, including the eye-rollers, Ms. Hildreth walks over to the board where she has posted a question related to the story she will use. "Today we'll work off the fairy tale 'The Three Little Pigs' again, and here is the question I'll be answering," the teacher says as she points to the prewritten question and reads it:

- If the First Little Pig learned his lesson in the story of "The Three Little Pigs," what materials would he use this time to build a new house?
- Why would he use these materials?
- Where might he build his new house?
- Be sure to include details from the story to support your answer.

"Oh, that's easy," responds Maria, ready to help her teacher compose the answer.

"And, you're not struggling," admonishes Fernando.

"I'm glad you're confident, Maria! And Fernando, just be patient. You know, the reason we use fairy tales is that they help us learn the processes in a comfortable way," the teacher explains. "Today I want to introduce a demonstration technique called think-aloud and write-aloud, which is exactly what it sounds like: a lesson where I tell you—I think aloud—what's in my head. Then, as I am writing, I am again saying aloud what I am writing or thinking. We'll call them TAWAs.

"Did you ever wonder what was in a teacher's head?" the teacher asks. "Well, you'll get to see how sometimes when I think and when I write, I get all jumbled up and have to step back or revise my thinking and my writing. At least that is what I think you'll see, because I have not practiced this, so who knows what might happen! I haven't planned what I'm going to say, so you may even find it humorous that your teacher would have to go back and forth so many times. I'll probably stammer and stutter—and struggle, Fernando, so be patient and just watch, okay? Everybody ready?"

The students nod their heads, with faces that show an interest in what is about to take place. So, Ms. Hildreth announces, "Here goes . . ." and all eyes follow her lead.

The first thing she does is to read the entire question aloud. Then she ponders, "Let me see. I want to restate the question first, so I am writing . . ." As she speaks, she moves into a write-aloud, saying each word as she writes: "*If the First Little Pig learned his lesson in the story of 'The Three Little Pigs'*—now, I don't want to use *what*" she says, pointing back at the question, "because that is a question word and this is the answer, so, let's see. I could say *the materials would*—no, I don't want to say *the materials would*, I want to say *the materials he would use this time . . . to build a new house are*—no, wait. I am not sure if I want to say *are* because then I have to say more than one kind of material— plural. I kind of think the pigs would use bricks. Is bricks? Are bricks? Yes! I do want it to be *are bricks*."

The teacher then decides to reread, "So far, I have *If the First Little Pig learned his lesson in the story of 'The Three Little Pigs,' the materials he would use to build a new house are bricks.*

"No! *Would be bricks*," she adds, revising again, and then suddenly remembering something else, she sighs, "Uh-oh, I still have those other questions to consider, so I better read them to see if I want to restate them right now or later in a different paragraph." So, the teacher again rereads the question parts, "Why would he use these materials? Where might he build his new house? Be sure to include details from the story to support your answer. Hm-m-m. I think I should begin my next sentence with the why question, but I won't exactly have to restate it. Maybe . . . like . . . *He would build his new house out of bricks because*—yes, *why* usually goes with *because.*

"Let me read it from the beginning again and see if it sounds right. *If the First Little Pig learned his lesson in the story of 'The Three Little Pigs,' the materials he would use to build his new house would be bricks. He would build his new house out of bricks because*—Okay. Why would he build his house out of bricks? 'What do you mean by this?' the Stranger would ask me.

"I'm going to jot down some things from the story on this other piece of chart paper, because I have to keep in mind that it said to use details from the story to support my answer. So-o-o-o-o . . . in the story

58

Better Answers

it said that the First Pig built his first house out of straw, but then the wolf blew it in," Ms. Hildreth says as she employs a write-aloud of brief notes: *1st pig / straw / wolf blew in*.

Then, she continues to read and present through the TAWA technique, "His brother, the Second Pig, built his house out of sticks, and the wolf blew that over, too." And, she writes while saying, *2nd, sticks, w. blew over*.

"So, both of those houses would not be good because they can be blown over easily," Ms. Hildreth says, moving back into a think-aloud.

"But, the Third Pig built his house out of bricks, and the wolf could not blow his house over, no matter how hard he tried," and she jots a few notes again on the chart paper: *3rd, bricks, YES! W. did not blow over!*

"Okay, but wait, the wolf could come down his chimney, so maybe the best house would have no chimney," and again at the chart she writes *Chimney = problem. No chimney?*

"Well, no . . . that wouldn't work because I think chimneys always have to have an open hole—or do they? I don't know. So, I better not use that. But, he could put something with holes over the chimney so the smoke could get out and the wolf could not get in. Yes, I remember that when we had birds coming in our fireplace in the springtime, we had to put this wire mesh over the chimney. Then the smoke got out, but the birds couldn't come in," she says, turning to the chart again and writing: *wire over chimney?* And, thinking aloud, she reminds both the class and herself, "I won't be putting anything from my own personal experience in this!

"Now, maybe I am ready to write the details. Let's see . . ." And, the teacher rereads her incomplete answer one more time: *If the First Little Pig learned his lesson in the story of 'The Three Little Pigs,' the materials he would use to build his new house would be bricks. He would build his new house out of bricks because* . . . because . . . I cannot say anything just yet about the bad straw and the bad sticks. I have to tell why the bricks are good first. Okay . . . *He would build his new house out of bricks because bricks are very strong.* Hm-m-m. *They are stronger than many other materials*—No, wait." (The teacher crosses out the sentence beginning.) "I want to use details from the story, so I will write *The Third Pig built his house out of bricks and when the wolf came he could not blow it down.* There! Details from the story to show that bricks are strong. But, now I'm probably going to need a transition word . . . Hm-m-m-m. Whereas? Yes! *Whereas . . . the First Pig built his house out of straw and the wolf was able to blow it right down, so straw would not be a good building material.* Yes, I'm on a roll now. *Furthermore,* Great connector! *Furthermore*" the teacher repeats with a kind of exaggerated, elitist sophistication in her voice, "*the Second Pig built his house out of sticks, and the wolf was able to blow that one down, also.*

"Now I think I can add the ending sentence. Oops! No! The chimney screen. Maybe I will start this one with . . . *Also, he may want to make sure there is a screen or something so smoke can—*No, that won't work because the sentence will be too long. Let me see. *Also, he may want to make sure there is . . .* is . . . something on the chimney hole . . . to let the smoke out, but . . . but, but, keep the wolf from getting in.

"Okay. The paragraph ending. I'm going to look back at the first part and restate it again. Let's see. I think I could write, *That is why the First Pig would choose bricks this time.* Good! 'That is why'—right from the Better Answer Sandwich. Good ending!

"Now, I'll read that whole paragraph over to make sure it sounds right." Ms. Hildreth goes on to reread the paragraph, and just as she thinks she is finished, she exclaims, "Wait. I'm not done because there is another part to the question: Where might he build his new house? I better restate that new question and start a whole new paragraph, because I just ended the last one. Let's see . . .

"*The First Pig might build his new house—*Where? Where would he build it? Where did the others build their houses? Well, they were close enough that they could run to each other's houses when they were in trouble. But, when they ran to the Third Pig's house it sounded like they just made it. Maybe I should have them live really close together. It said I had to use details from the story and there weren't many details about where they built their houses. There weren't any pictures, either. Maybe I could answer using those few details the author did give, and then at the very end add only one other sentence that would come from my own head about where a good place would be. Just to add a touch of voice right at the end. But, I will have to be careful because the person who made up this question wants me to use only details from the story." So, the teacher continues to write aloud.

"*The First Pig might build his new house . . . he might build his new house . . . close to the other two pigs—*No, wait. I'm going to say" (and the teacher strikes out the last six words) "*close to his family.* Yes! Too many pig words in here!" she says, and giving a little snort, glances over her glasses at the class with a smirk that invites humor into the moment.

"Okay, so now I have to tell why—using details from the story. *The First Pig might build his new house close to his family,*" Ms. Hildreth rereads. "I'm not going to put a *because* this time. I'll use supporting details in the very next sentence instead. *The First Pig might build his new house close to his family. When the wolf almost caught him and his brother, they ran to the next house to be safe.* Okay. So what? They ran to the next house. So what? the Stranger would ask. If the next house had been farther away, the wolf would have caught them. Connecting word. Connecting word? *Therefore, the First Pig would build his house very close to*—Use a synonym. Say *family* in a different way. *Therefore, the First Pig would build his house close to . . . those who love him and . . . and, and . . . will take care of him if he gets into trouble, just like The Third Little Pig did.* Good. Now. An ending for this paragraph . . . and maybe for the whole thing.

"Let's see. I'll go back and reread the key question again before I decide how to end this. If the First Little Pig learned his lesson in the story of 'The Three Little Pigs,' what materials would he use this time to build a new house? Why would he use these materials?

"Well . . . maybe I will add just a touch of my own opinion here at the end—but not too much. Just enough to add some voice to this writing," she thinks aloud and then goes on into a TAWA: "*I hope that both the First Pig and the Second Pig did learn their lesson because . . . because . . . because . . . if they did not . . . they may not live to . . . to . . . to . . . to tell the tale again.* Yes! That's good!" the teacher exclaims and then rereads the whole sentence: "*I hope that both the First Pig and the Second Pig did learn their lesson because if they did not they may not live to tell the tale again.* But, I cannot have a one-sentence paragraph, so I can either move it up into the last paragraph or add more. I guess maybe I will just move it up into the last paragraph."

At this point, the teacher rereads the questions and then the entire piece aloud, eliminates a couple of words, then turns to the group, and asks, "Questions?"

Several students respond by suggesting what she could have added to the piece. The teacher agrees with them, but later explains, "You know, there are a million correct ways this could have been written. I'm glad you have good ideas, too. I'll let you use your own ideas on a new one tomorrow. We'll do buddy-sharing and you can do a TAWA from the new question with your partners. Like what I did with you today. But, right now it is time for lunch!"

It is really quite amazing how students are scaffolded forward through this kind of think-aloud/write-aloud experience. Yet, it should not be so surprising that when we make covert processes overt, students readily learn them, because we let the secret out of the bag.

There are a number of other ways to help students develop a more reflective attitude about the details they are including to support their answers. Some of these follow.

Inviting the Stranger into Student TAWAs

Kids are great mimics! As a matter of fact, that is the main way we learn: by watching others. Why not take advantage of this?

After demonstrating a few think- and write-aloud lessons, partner students, present the dyads with a fairly easy extended-response question, and ask them to take turns playing the teacher-demonstrator. That is, one partner begins thinking aloud through writing while the other partner listens. At the end of that sentence, the other partner shares the pen to continue the answer. Each partner must listen carefully to the other; if he does not, he will have trouble when it is his turn.

Afterward, they draw straws to see who will take the part of the Stranger, investigating the collaborative work to see if it makes sense and can stand alone. They love this activity and it's even worth all the noise it creates!

Using the Answer Scale to Defend a Piece

After students respond to a question, ask them to score their pieces on the Better Answer scale. Then invite them to defend those scores with a partner by providing related evidence. That is, students should actually take their partners back into the text to read aloud the supporting section.

The teacher will have to demonstrate this process the first couple of times, using her own work, so that students can follow her lead. Without teacher modeling, students will respond in myriad ways, which may or may not be supportive. So, modeling is mandatory here.

I usually begin by using a previous piece from a TAWA, running through each part of the Better Answer scale, explaining my reasoning for each part as it relates to my piece of writing. I begin with, "I restated the question because the question was . . . and I used the following words . . . I gave a gist answer for the question because I said . . . and that answer was not specific, but still gave a kind of basic answer." I carry on in the same fashion through the other parts of the scale.

When I finish, I share a couple of pieces from an old state assessment or take the selections off the Internet sites that have benchmarked pieces. I invite partners to collaborate and then share as we decide whether the evidence is there or not. Finally, I invite partners to share their responses with each other in a similar fashion while I tour the room, scaffolding where it is needed.

Afterward, students should be offered a period of time in which to edit or revise. It's important they know early on that they will eventually have this revision opportunity. Otherwise, they tend to stop midstream to insert omitted words, erase spelling errors, and such—which of course bores the listener.

Ordering Importance

ACTIVITY

When students judge the level of importance of each piece of selected information, they must come to grips with the fact that some information is definitely more important than others. And, to add depth to this, it is even better to have them defend their leveled placement of each piece of information.

It's helpful, at least the first few times, to take the reading and selection process off the students' shoulders by doing a read-aloud with all important information *already* underlined. Afterward, common forms (copies) with the underlining are distributed for partners to order.

But, before they can order the underlined parts, a question about the text is displayed. Partners are asked to order each piece, relating its relevance to the answer. They then cut each strip of information apart and decide where it belongs on a list called Most Important to Least Important Information. Having them work together encourages those with different opinions to defend their stances. This is exactly what we are hoping for, that is, for students to be able to articulate why one fact is more important than another.

After partners finish the task, a whole-group meeting will add another interesting dimension to the issue of most important/least important. However, what we anticipate is that students will come to understand that within each article or essay read, there is some information that will stand head and shoulders above the rest to support a particular answer.

I have also written the important details on sentence strips, which can then be moved in a different order as we talk about them in a whole-class situation. Being able to move writing around is very helpful to some students who tend to follow the motto Once it's down, it's down! It relieves us of some of writing's permanence and actually encourages revision. It can also serve as a prewriting strategy that might then actually eliminate revision.

On-Topic/Off-Topic

ACTIVITY

This activity begins as many of the others, with a brief, curriculum-correlated article, essay, or story that is read aloud to the students, but this time they have the text to follow along. Afterward, a question related to that piece is displayed where it can be seen throughout the rest of the lesson.

Each student has two large cards: one on which he has written ON-TOPIC in large letters and the other on which he has OFF-TOPIC. From her curriculum-related question prompt the teacher has composed an answer, one that maintains the topic most of the time, but occasionally strays off course onto something that is not necessarily closely related. She reads a bit of this answer, and then stops to ask, "Off-topic or on-topic?" Each student should then respond by displaying the related card. Each time, after she stops for a show of cards, the teacher goes back to repeat the process at another spot in the answer.

This activity can be transferred to later lessons, when the students share their independently constructed answers with partners instead of with the teacher. That is, in a gamelike fashion, they can respond to their partner's sentences with the related card.

ASSESSING CONFERRING

Assessment Type: Topic Checklist

During this step I present a rather simple checklist to help students evaluate the veracity of their details. This checklist asks only three questions, but students must sign off on each before sharing work with me or anyone else.

Sometimes I have them partner, read their complete answers to each other, and then discuss the answer to each of these questions together.

Focus Questions

This time the questions are the students' and can be asked of themselves or their partner:

- Did I prove my answer?
- Does what I wrote make sense? (And, did I reread to see if it did?)
- What would the Stranger ask me about what I wrote?

The Answer's Readableness

By this point, the content is lookin' good and the kids are soundin' smart. Most students are now ready to focus on the conventions of the piece, the grammar, spelling, punctuation, capitalization, and first and foremost, the handwriting. Why handwriting first? Read on.

Use Proper Conventions

Conventions do not determine what an author writes. Intentions determine what an author wishes to say, and conventions permit it to be said. Conventions offer the means of expressing an intention.

(Smith 1982, p. 92)

What Are Conventions?

Conventions include the signs, symbols, and form through which the writer conveys a message. They are obviously important, for they invite the reader into the content. Yet, without content, grammar, punctuation, spelling, and such become little more than marks on paper. For that reason, I leave the conventions for the last step, that is, after the content is in place.

I want students to have fully conceived pieces before we get into cosmetics. That's the way I handle it in my own writing in the real world, as well. Most authors do wait, because conventions don't matter much when a piece is poorly conceived. Nonetheless, it is through the window of conventions that we are able to discern the content.

Under the conventions heading, I include everything that relates to the overt readableness of a piece. Indeed, this is no small consideration. There are tons of books devoted to the teaching of conventions. Entire volumes have been written about grammar alone. But, to address the issue of readableness of any given piece, I again begin with simplicity and reality.

I suggest that the most important aspect of conventions is the overt appearance of the piece, that is, what the eye sees even before it attempts to decode the content. I speak here of spacing and smudges, legibility, and sharpened pencils. What will the reader's preconceived notion be—even before he or she actually begins to read the piece?

Avenues for Teaching Writing Conventions

Keeping Responses Legible and Neat

It seems logical then, to begin with the issue of handwriting and neatness. Why do I believe handwriting and neatness are so important? Because, if the handwriting is a mess or the paper is smudged, the reader is inclined to feel that the content is probably a mess. Thus, we strive here to lay the groundwork for only the most positive preconceived notions.

I explain the poignancy of literary cosmetics by revealing the impact of sloppy handwriting on the real world. I tell students that on employment applications and important tests, those who have neat paperwork with legible handwriting are more apt to come out on top. As a matter of fact, a teacher in our district had a number of students write exactly the same answer, but she told half of them to write using sloppy handwriting, while the others she asked to write very neatly. She then gave the papers to teachers throughout the school to correct. Invariably, the neat papers received better scores—even though the answers were exactly the same, except for the quality of handwriting.

When I tell the kids this true story, I also tell them that this is not mean or evil. It's life. Sad, but true: People judge on appearances. I like to be up front with kids, because they appreciate that kind of honesty, and they pass it on to their friends, as well.

In our focus on handwriting I emphasize that it is not so much the shape of each alphabet letter, but more a matter of spacing words and letters and keeping the quantity of erasures limited. In other words, neatness matters.

The mere act of beginning by indenting, a somewhat mindless habit that can be easily instilled, makes a student look smart. Most teachers tend to have students use a two-finger indenting width before they begin writing. When kids indent—especially struggling students—I celebrate, "Wow! You're lookin' smart with that wide-space indenting!"

I place a similar importance on keeping to evenly placed beginnings for each line on the page. These are easy to accomplish, but can have a major effect on the overall result. Furthermore, these strategies help students feel like they have control over their products.

Other Conventions

Here we are at a place where teachers often display their most negative predictions: "There is no way you are going to get Maria to spell correctly!" or "Say what you want, Natasha Smith will never learn where periods belong!"

I must say that when I began working with that group of struggling fifth graders, I too thought, "Whatever I do, I cannot see how I will ever get them to use acceptable conventions!" I had tried for a year to get Joey to use periods, but he *still* did not use them! And I figured he probably never would. However, I was wrong. Very wrong.

My explanation for how that group of students moved over the conventions hump is this: When they first began to use the Better Answer formula, they wrote very little—just two or three sentences. They wore their defeatist attitudes like a gray veil, and this affected everything they did. Once they understood how to restate and answer the question, however, their attitudes began to change and the veil lifted. Their confidence grew. And, by the time they were filling the page with details, it seemed to me that they had also begun to see themselves in a new light. I truly believe that they decided that if they could do all that, they were not going to allow conventions to hold them back.

Their final products therefore often had near-perfect conventions, especially compared with the initial pieces they had produced. I was taken aback as much as you will be. With that said, let's move on to some strategies.

Monitoring Progress Using Spreadsheets and Student Folders

It was really helpful when I was a reading teacher to keep an ongoing spreadsheet on which I logged all students along the vertical axis and the seven parts of the Better Answer scale along the horizontal. I could quickly check the spreadsheet for grouping purposes, as well as for individual conference purposes. When a teacher or parent wanted to know how a particular student was progressing, that spreadsheet held up-to-date information. Appendix E of this book contains some examples for reference and some templates for classroom use.

Furthermore, I kept a folder of samples of student work onto which was stapled a marked Better Answer scale. It held an at-a-glance assessment of that piece. Each month the student and I selected another piece of work that would show growth. We placed the sample in the folder and logged the results on the spreadsheet. Many times that system became a handy tool for ready access. If a student's attitude waned defeatist, I would pull out his progress sheet and his ongoing samples of response writing, and we would together follow the growth he had made. His attitude wound would heal and he'd be back in writing mode before I had a chance to refile his folder.

There are a number of other instructional avenues that seemed to work for us. They helped students improve their spelling, grammar, punctuation, and capitalization.

ACTIVITY

Editing at the Ends of Lines

When time or number of students limit us from having individual conferences and we must take students' papers home to review, it is beneficial to place error marks at the ends of lines, rather than above or on an error. For the better students, I merely put a check mark; if there are two errors, I put two check marks at the end of the line. For struggling students, I place a more revealing mark, such as "sp." for spelling, or "p." for punctuation. Regardless, students must identify errors and edit accordingly.

I remember when my own children would bring home their school writing upon which the teacher had strategically corrected all their errors. The only times they noticed the teacher's corrections were when I drew their attention to them or when they had to copy their work over. Even then it was a mindless endeavor. In other words, they were not actually learning anything and would probably make the same errors again. In fact, they did.

When we mark at the ends of lines, however, the students themselves must investigate where the errors lie and repair them. In the process of each search, they are learning.

The first time I use end-marks and return the papers to the students, it is helpful and less time-consuming to have them partner, so they can collaboratively find and edit errors. After they understand the operation, they can undertake the task independently. Because the emphasis here appears to be on errors, I must add that each paper also contains an equitable quantity of positive remarks.

Celebrating Small Improvements

It never ceases to amaze me how a kind word here or there can work wonders. So, I look for the "good stuff"—and nothing is too small to be celebrated. Although this area is important enough to deserve thirty pages, suffice it to say that the mere act of holding a teaching certificate connotes a level of kindness and caring. We need to put that kindness out in front—always.

Why not invite the kids into the kindness circle, as well? Take five minutes now and then to invite students to trade papers with someone and then find every good thing they can about that person's response. They can jot these brief compliments on a sticky note that can be placed atop the paper. I model it first and call it "Lookin' for the good stuff." Wouldn't it be great if this perspective carried over into other facets of life as well? Famous authors and artists tell of teachers they had who saw the good stuff in them when they could not see it in themselves.

The Spelling Dilemma

This is a tough one! How can a student who cannot spell do well on an assessment that evaluates spelling? A seeming conundrum.

One thing is sure: There are certain times, even for adults, when spelling will be a problem if we cannot use a dictionary. However, there are a few strategies that appear to help the struggling speller. We adults use these strategies, too, because we all become struggling spellers at times. Therefore, the following should sound familiar.

Spelling Strategies

Write It Five Ways
The first spelling strategy that I teach students when they are editing their essay's conventions is to write the questionable word in a number of ways on another piece of paper. "When the correct spelling pops out at you, use it," I say. "However, if you are still in doubt, do what we adults do," which is the second strategy I teach.

Use a Synonym
The second strategy is, if in doubt, use a synonym. Why take the chance of having a word marked wrong if there is a suitable synonym? I tell the

students, "If I have to jot a quick note to the principal or to a parent, and I'm not sure of the spelling of a word and have no time to look it up, you better believe I use a synonym!" The same thing happens often when an employee must write something to her superior. People in doubt who don't have a dictionary use a synonym.

A couple of mini-lessons is all students need to internalize this strategy. I sometimes think they especially like it because it seems like the teacher is suggesting they cheat! But I explain that it's not cheating—it's a real-life way to solve a spelling problem.

One last point regards spelling words in informal writing or rough drafts, that is, writing in journals or taking notes. It's important that students understand the difference between the risks we take on drafts and the risks we do *not* take on tests that score our spelling. In the real world, if we are being evaluated on a particular behavior, most adults are wise enough to monitor their risk-taking. Why shouldn't we teach kids to do the same thing?

Use What's Right There

Another obvious strategy that is sometimes overlooked involves using the question itself and other text information to spell correctly. This means that no restatement should be misspelled because the words are right there in the question. I tend to have a fit if students misspell words that are right there in print.

The real problem presents itself when the students must listen and respond *without* text, which does not happen quite so frequently; at least in school, it doesn't. However, some state assessments do have a listen-and-respond section. In this case, there are still words in the question that can be accessed for spelling reference. And, quite often proper nouns with multiple spellings, such as names, will be right there in the question. However, for other unknown spellings, the preceding two strategies often solve the problem.

Learn a High-Frequency Word List

The last and most time-consuming strategy concerns teaching students the high-frequency words that they are likely going to need. The Rebecca Sitton spelling program, based on the most commonly used words in student writing, is very helpful as an instructional sequence for struggling spellers. When students learn how to spell the words they use most frequently in their writing, it can have a dramatic influence.

Consider this: If students learn to spell the first 25 words on the Sitton list, they will be assured of having 33 percent of their writing spelled correctly; when they learn the first 100 words, they are assured of 68 percent correct. Focusing on the mastery of at least the first 100 or so words helps even the most challenged spellers to reach a higher level of competence.

The Rebecca Sitton web site can provide more information. Log on at http://www.curriculumassociates.com/authors/s.

Assessment Type: Using the Better Answer Scale to Confer

Once the students have the entire Better Answer formula under their belts, I confer in a way that conserves time. First of all, after students have responded in writing to a question from their reading, I take those papers home, staple a Better Answer scale to each one, and mark it according to the quality of the writing. Within the next few days (so that my aging mind does not lose track), I call each student over for a five-minute conference, focusing first on their 3s, that is, what they did well, and then on one area—just one area—in which I feel they could improve.

And here's the important part: I always zero in on the easiest-to-accomplish areas first. I make some suggestions for how they might improve in that area, and then I ask them the following question.

Focus Questions

The next time you construct an answer, what will your focus for improvement be and what strategy will you use for this?

It is prudent to use this question to evoke an exit commitment, because throughout the following week or two it can guide students toward better performance. They might even write their commitments down.

Classroom Vignette Demonstrating Steps 1 Through 5

This vignette takes place during a one-on-one conference, a time when the teacher has an opportunity to both celebrate the student's response and to scaffold him forward in one area. Notice how this teacher affirms Antonio's use of a conventions' strategy, but leaves him with a new strategy that will support his area of need.

Ms. Powers pulls Antonio's written response to yesterday's social studies task from the pile on her desk. She glances at the attached Better Answer scale scores as she invites Antonio to meet with her at the table on the side of the room. As teacher and student sit down beside each other, Ms. Powers smiles and compliments, "Antonio! You did much better this time on your social studies written-response task. Look at this," and she slides the paper in front of his two eager eyes.

Before Antonio has a chance to dwell on his mistakes, the teacher points to the positive areas of his paper and comments, "I was really pleased to see that both the restatement and the gist answer were perfect! I loved your top bun in the response.

"And, look at this! You scored a 3 in conventions this time! Only one tiny spelling error. Did you use any strategies that enabled you to do such a fine job on spelling this time?" Ms. Powers asks.

"I made sure I went back to the book spelling. You said we could use our books to spell, so I double-checked everything," Antonio responded somewhat proudly.

"Well, it sure paid off!" the teacher added. Then she went on to another aspect of the response.

"We can both see an area needing improvement, too," Ms. Powers reminds.

"Yeah, the details. I had trouble with those," the student confesses.

Ms. Powers thinks carefully about how she wants to address this issue so as not to evoke a defeatist attitude in Antonio, yet still develop a sound strategy for improvement. "Antonio, the thing I notice about your details is that, although you found three really good details, you did not explain them. You just kind of dropped them, as is, into the answer so that now they sound lost and lonely. They need an explanation to back them up.

"Let me read them to you," and the teacher reads aloud Antonio's answer. "The Mississippi River became an important body of water in the United States because it provided this country with a great natural resource. Its water has been used for travel, shipping, and power. That is why it is an important body of water.

"Antonio, in your answer I found out that the Mississippi is an important body of water because it is used for travel, shipping, and power, but what do you think I am wondering about that travel or shipping or power?" the teacher asked.

"I don't know. Maybe like where they travel . . . or maybe what gets shipped," Antonio responded.

"Sure! And, we talked all about those things. I knew you knew that. And, if you had told more about the travel, the shipping, and the power, you could easily have made your answer far richer and more informative. So, next time when you reread your answer, please look for your details and see if you have explained them enough so that some stranger would know what you meant. Okay?" Ms. Powers asked.

"Okay," Antonio answered with a shy smile.

"So, Antonio, what will you do next time you write a response?" the teacher asks, encouraging a commitment statement from the student.

"I'm gonna look at my details and see if I told enough so that the Stranger would know what I mean," he responds.

"Great! I can't wait to read your next response. It's gonna be even better than this one! Tap Sam on the shoulder as you pass his desk, please. I need him next," Ms. Powers requests as she reaches for another paper from the pile, and Antonio leaves the table.

Will This Protocol Work in Every Classroom?

The Better Answer formula is much like any other process we teach or are taught. If it is implemented daily across the curriculum, it will have a major impact on student performance. However, if it is mentioned briefly here and there, the effects will be far less notable.

Therefore, I suggest you use this protocol often. The students love it because it empowers them. Teachers tell me again and again that it builds confidence—probably the major missing ingredient in those who perform poorly in school, on the job, anywhere.

However, the Better Answer formula is only the beginning. It is the mere framework upon which students will build deeper, richer responses rooted in multiple genres from a variety of subjects. Eventually, we'll barely be able to see that framework undergirding their exquisite and captivating responses.

Afterword
What Comes Next?

Not long ago, I pondered whether I really wanted to write this book. It bothered me that it did not unfold much beyond an initial framework or formula. But then I decided that initial steps are a very valid entry point to all learning, and I have worked with enough teachers to know that they surely will not let the buck stop with Chapter 5 of this book. Once they get kids over the hump and into acceptable responses, those teachers will move beyond the bare bones structures of the Better Answer formula. When they do, each teacher's "afterword" will unfold in its own way, but I surely hope it includes some common and essential elements.

Mindful teachers will immerse their students in the reading of real essays while inviting them to grapple with related issues. Their students will compare essays' grand variety of forms, and afterward, students will emulate the standards of those authors they've read. To set such teachers on this journey, I developed a bibliography of resources, which is included in Appendix E of this book. There you will find a raft of essay/article sources to support your commitment to those next steps.

When mindful teachers nurture students away from the formula's focus on tales and into its applications, they'll first use brief and very interesting essays by authors their students will recognize. That is, they'll ignite curiosity and interest by selecting essays from authors like Steve Young,

Shaquille O'Neal, Jim Brown, Jack Kemp, and Bill Cosby, all of whom have published in the *Chicken Soup for the Soul* (Canfield and Hansen 1993 and others) books. Furthermore, many of these *Chicken Soup* essays correlate well with our curricular intentions. For instance, they include authors such as Helen Keller, Roald Dahl, Gloria Steinem, Theodore Roosevelt, Ralph Waldo Emerson, Rudyard Kipling, and Viktor E. Frankl. Such texts demonstrate the real reasons that people write response essays.

The scaffolding into these more complex texts will occur with grace and finesse if each step forward includes articles and essays that maintain a high level of student interest. Give your students the gift of authentic text—texts that correlate with your curriculum, but remain richer and far more exciting than textbooks and, most obviously, workbooks; authentic writing written by "real" people grappling with "real" issues; texts that coax kids to turn on and tune in.

Eventually, many teachers will invite students to investigate the authentic essays of young people just like themselves—kids who have found their voice and their cause and who have published their essays in magazines and paperbacks such as *Teen Ink,* and *Taste Berries for Teens.* Some teachers will take this a step farther and invite their students to contribute to these ongoing publications. They'll show their kids how to go online and publish their critical review of a CD or book on the Barnes and Noble or Amazon web site. Yes, teachers who understand what writing is all about will invite their students to construct essays for real-world purposes, to publish their work, to be committed to causes, to be heard.

Offer your students real essay writers to emulate. Offer them real issues to question. Offer them real causes for which they feel compelled to write responses. Offer your kids a tool through which they can help change the world. Offer them authentic essay responses. For indeed, this is what essay writing is all about. It's not about tests in school.

Essay writing is about citizens who care enough to pick up the pen and write. Their authentic response says, this is who I am, and this is why I feel this way; this is what I know, and I think you should know it, too.

Just as the Better Answer formula is a basic framework, a first step into response writing, so should answers constructed on performance assessments be a first step. But, we teachers cannot stop there! When kids are immersed in a curriculum of rich and real essay and response writing, they will approach today's detached, standardized assessments reveling in the confidence that can be created only by reading and writing for real purposes. Indeed, they will know how to look good and sound smart, not only on tests, but also in real life.

Six Fairy Tales and Fables with Questions and Petition Prompts

Contents

The following are retold by Ardith Davis Cole.
"Little Red Riding Hood"
"The Three Little Pigs"
"Goldilocks and the Three Bears"
"The Grasshopper and the Ants"
"The Lion and the Mouse"
"The City Mouse and the Country Mouse"

The following fairy tales and fables were constructed to provide ready access to simplistic text. Most of this book's examples are rooted in one of these short stories. Their availability will make it easy for teachers to use the methodology, the texts, and their prompts while using the Better Answer formula in their own classrooms.

The fairy tales ("Little Red Riding Hood," "The Three Little Pigs," and "Goldilocks and the Three Bears") are presented at a somewhat more sophisticated level to accommodate the interest of middle school students; whereas, the fables maintain a much lower level of readability. Yet, both would work with most students in order to demonstrate written response processes. The fables ("The Grasshopper and the Ants," "The Lion and the Mouse," and "The City Mouse and the Country Mouse") are especially handy when time is limited, for their brevity accommodates our overly packed curricula. Actually, any of Aesop's very common fables will suit our purpose.

Following the set of tales you will find a set of questions and petitions that can be used as prompts during modeling. Certainly, other possibilities abound, but the busy teacher may appreciate that everything needed for modeling is right in this book.

Little Red Riding Hood

Retold by Ardith Davis Cole

On the edge of a deep, dark woods there lived a woodcutter, his wife, and their young daughter. The little girl loved to frolic in the surrounding forest, which was often quite a bit cooler and more damp than her yard. For that reason her mother made her a beautiful red, hooded cape to keep her warm and dry. The child loved the cloak and wore it daily, regardless of the weather. Consequently, everyone called her Little Red Riding Hood.

One day Little Red Riding Hood's mother said to her, "Grandmother is not feeling well, so I'd like you to take this basket of goodies to her, please. Stay on the path and do not dawdle along the way. I must stay home, for the horse is very ill and needs my attention."

Little Red Riding Hood's grandmother lived at the end of a long forest path. The little girl had made the trip numerous times before, but always with her mother or father. However, she loved the walk and was not one bit frightened, as many other children may have been.

Carefully carrying her basket so as not to spill its contents, she skipped along, singing a merry melody. Suddenly, there appeared before her a large wolf, who at first startled the little girl; however, never having met a wolf before, she relaxed quickly when he offered a kind greeting. "Good morning, little girl. Where might you be going on this beautiful summer day?"

"I'm taking food to Grandmother. She is not feeling well. Mother says that this basket of goodies will pick up her spirits. Where are you going, sir?" the little girl asked in turn.

"Oh, no place really. I'm just enjoying the day. Where does your grandmother live?" the old conniver continued.

"At the end of the path in a little pink cottage," she answered, but then remembered what her mother had told her. "I'd better go along now because Mother said I shouldn't dawdle. Bye," she said as she naively started on her way once more.

"Good-bye, little girl," responded the wolf, ducking back into the bushes and then darting off, intent on reaching Grandmother's house before Little Red Riding Hood. He had plans for that little girl—plans that included dinner.

Therefore, unbeknownst to Little Red Riding Hood the wolf arrived at Grandmother's house considerably before the child. He pulled her grandmother out of bed, tied her up, and locked her in the back shed. Then, he found one of the grandmother's nightgowns and her frilly cap, put them on, and crawled under the bedcovers, which he pulled up so as to reveal only his large, bushy, wolf eyes.

Before long, there was a quiet knock at the door. Knowing it was the child, the wolf called in a falsetto that mimicked an elderly woman, "Come in."

Little Red Riding Hood thought that her grandmother sounded very ill, so she anxiously opened the door and rushed to her bedside. She began disassembling the basket to show her grandmother all the wonderful items Mother had packed. Eventually, the child looked up and could not help but gasp, "Grandmother! What big eyes you have!"

"The better to see you with, my dear," answered the wolf in his most grandmotherly voice.

"But . . . but . . . but Grandmother, what big ears you have, too," the bewildered child whispered.

"The better to hear you with, my dear," responded the wolf, this time more excitedly. His impatience took its toll, for the bedcovers slipped down a bit, exposing his nose and mouth.

"And, Grandmother! What big TEETH you have!" Little Red Riding Hood screamed, now fearing the worst.

"The better to EAT you with," snapped the wolf hungrily, as he bounded from the bed and snatched the little girl within the blink of an eye.

"And now, dinner!" he exclaimed, licking his chops.

"Help! Help! Help!" shouted Little Red Riding Hood at the top of her lungs. But, by this time the wolf was charging pell-mell back into the woods with the child securely in tow. She kicked and she punched, but try as she might, the wolf was her superior in strength.

Just then, out of the forest depths came Little Red Riding Hood's father and two other woodsmen. Seeing their axes, the wolf dropped the little girl on the path and took off like an Olympic racer. But, he was not quite fast enough because, as the crafty old animal flew by, one woodcutter managed to remove the wolf's tail.

"Oo-oo-oo!" that old devil cried, as he created distance between himself and his pursuers.

Within seconds, the wolf's cries blended with the cries of another. "It's Grandmother!" celebrated Little Red Riding Hood. "She's alive!" And they all ran in the direction of the muffled cries.

Soon, the grateful group was all together again, unharmed. "It's time to put my real grandmother back to bed," announced Little Red Riding Hood, "because I think we've seen the last of that awful old animal, but just in case he needs a reminder—" At that point Little Red Riding Hood hung the wolf's tail, which she had been carrying, on a nail by the cottage door. And there it remains to this very day.

The Three Little Pigs

Retold by Ardith Davis Cole

Once upon a time there were three little pigs who lived together with their mother in the home where they were born. From dusk to dawn the brothers played together, until the day came when their mother said to them, "Little pigs, you are not so little anymore. It is time for you to go out into the world and seek your fortunes."

The three were excited about the possibilities before them. "We'll travel the world!" shouted the first little pig.

"I'll find a wife!" exclaimed the second pig.

But the third and more sensible pig reminded, "Not so fast. We have to first put a roof over our heads. We must build a home where we will be safe, where we can stay warm when it's cold, where we can raise a family."

"He's right," grumbled the dejected first pig. "Let's get started so we can investigate the more interesting aspects of life."

So, each pig set forth, intent on the goal of building his own house. The first pig was finished quickly, for he built his house from bales of straw he had purchased from a nearby farmer. The second little pig finished shortly after the first, for he had built his shelter of sticks, most of which he'd gathered from the neighborhood, as well as the woods. Both pigs were proud of their efficient ingenuity and were very pleased that they would soon be able to engage in the more exciting facets of life.

However, the third little pig developed a different plan. He decided to build his house out of bricks. He wanted a house that would last forever, one that would keep him safe from any harm. Bricks would make a mighty fortress, he thought. Unfortunately, this would not be an easy task. Each small brick would have to be shaped and dried. Furthermore, it would take considerable effort and time to lay all of them once they were ready. But, the third pig was determined, and brick by brick his house took shape.

Sometimes his brothers went to watch their industrious sibling work. Pig 3 enjoyed their company, but he did not enjoy their teasing. "Think he'll be done by the time he's old and gray?" joshed Pig 2.

"Nah!" responded Pig 1. "It'll take a lifetime." Then, they'd roll on the ground laughing.

Better Answers

Next, they'd try to dissuade Pig 3's intentions. "Come on, Pig 3," nudged Pig 1, "just use straw to finish it. You're making it difficult when it could be so easy." But, the third pig was adamant and continued on, brick by brick. Eventually, he did finish.

It so happened that one day, not long after Pig 3 had completed his project, Pig 1 had a visitor. The first little pig heard a knock on the door, so he glanced out the window to see who it was. "Oh, no!" he gasped. "A wolf!" Trying to put off the seemingly inevitable, Pig 1 asked in a polite voice, "Who's there?"

The wolf also disguised his voice and answered, "It is I, your kind neighbor."

Unable to contain himself, the little pig shouted, "You're not my neighbor! You are a wolf! Go away!"

However, the wolf would not be thwarted, but instead continued, "Little pig, little pig, let me come in."

"Not by the hairs on my chinny-chin-chin," stuttered Pig 1.

"Then I'll huff, and I'll puff, and I'll BLOW your house in!" And, that mean old wolf did exactly as he said he would do. Of course it did not take long to level a straw house.

Fortunately for Pig 1, he had dashed out the back door just in time and ran as fast as his little pig legs would carry him to the house of Pig 2. He darted through the front door, bolting it behind him. Pig 2 was startled by Pig 1's behavior, and responded accordingly, "What's going on, for goodness sake?"

"It-It-It's the wolf," stammered Pig 1, out of breath. "He blew my house down!" The words no sooner left his lips than there came a boisterous pounding at the bolted door.

"Little pigs, little pigs, let me come in!" demanded the wolf.

The two pigs hugged each other, and with trembling voices replied in unison, "Not by the hairs on our chinny-chin-chins."

"Then I'll huff, and I'll puff, and I'll blow this house in!" declared the wolf. The pigs did not wait to see what might happen, but instead dashed out the back door and headed as fast as their pig legs could carry them to the third brother's home.

After the wolf had huffed and puffed and puffed and huffed enough to bring down the stick house, he discovered his predetermined dinner was gone. Thus, his temper was raging when he vowed, "I'll have piggy pie for supper yet. They'll not escape this next time."

Meanwhile, Pig 1 and Pig 2 ran into the arms of their brother, who was stunned, but sympathetic. Out of breath and sobbing, they implored Pig 3 to bolt the door and secure the house, for the wolf was on their trail. Calmly, Pig 3 replied, "Sit down in my nice soft chairs, brothers. I'll take care of this bothersome lout." With that, he picked up a large kettle of water and placed it over the flame in the fireplace.

All too soon, there came a most disruptive banging on the door, followed by, "Little pigs, little pigs, let me come in."

Huddled together, the three pigs sang out at the top of their lungs, "Not by the hairs on our chinny-chin-chins."

"Then I'll huff and I'll puff and I'll blow your house in!" roared the wolf.

"Oh no, you won't blow a brick house over, Mr. Wolf! There is no way for you to get into this house except for the chimney—and it is too high," the third pig called deceivingly.

So the wolf huffed and puffed until he was all out of breath, but he just could not move one brick in Pig 3's house. But then, he remembered!

"Ha!" responded the wolf under his breath. "They think I can't get up there. Just watch." With that, the wolf pulled a ladder—a leftover remnant from building the house—over to the far wall, positioned it carefully, and began his journey upward. With a hungry smile on his face, the conniving canine entered the chimney. Down he went, down, down, down . . . right into a large kettle of boiling water. Splash!

"Yow!" he screamed, and flew straight back up the chimney. He skipped the ladder and rolled to the ground, vowing never to approach that family of pigs again. And, the last the pigs saw of the wolf were his soggy footprints heading in the direction of the animal burn clinic.

Goldilocks and the Three Bears

Retold by Ardith Davis Cole

There was once a little girl whose curls sparkled like gold. For that reason, everyone called her Goldilocks. This adventuresome, energetic child lived with her mother and father near a large, dense forest.

Now, Goldilocks's mother was a fearful sort and was forever cautioning her only child to be careful. She especially worried about the nearby forest, where she was certain all sorts of wild animals lurked, waiting to gobble up her sweet little girl. However, that very same woods appeared inviting to the young child, beckoning her to visit, explore, and play along its paths.

Therefore, one day when her mother was consumed with housework, Goldilocks scampered off to investigate the world outside her yard. Before long, she found herself amidst the birds and branches, the bugs and bushes—an interesting place, indeed. As she scurried along, noticing this and that, her attention was drawn to a small cottage in a clearing.

In that cottage lived three bears: Mama, Papa, and Baby. That same morning, as the bears were waiting for their porridge to cool, Baby Bear began to beg, "Walk? Walk? Walk?" So, Mama and Papa decided to let their breakfasts cool and grant Baby Bear her request.

So it was that when Goldilocks stood on tippy-toes to look in the cottage windows, there was no one to be seen. She next went to the entryway, and when she touched the door to knock, it opened a little. Considering this an invitation, she peeked inside. "Hello," she called out, but received no response.

"Hello-o-o-o!" she sang, this time a bit louder. But, still no one answered. So, she pushed the door ajar and walked into the cottage's cheerful kitchen.

When the little girl spotted the three bowls of porridge on the table, she realized how very hungry she was after her long walk. At first, she just sniffed, taking in the rich warmth of the cereal. But, when she could no longer resist, she tasted of the biggest bowl. "Oh! Too hot!" she cried to no one.

Having learned from Papa Bear's very hot bowl, she immediately noticed the steam rising from Mama Bear's bowl and thus circumvented it, as well. However, the third tiny bowl had no steam, and once she tried it, Goldilocks consumed the entire bowl in just a few minutes.

With the cavity in her belly now filled, the little girl ventured into the next room. There sat three chairs—one very large one, one midsized, and, in the far corner, a cute baby's rocking chair decorated with colorful flowers. Goldilocks decided to test the little one, but became so zealous in her rocking that she soon found herself on the floor with the chair around her in pieces. Disappointed, she tried to reconstruct the pieces—alas, to no avail.

By this time, she was becoming very tired, for the walk had been a long one. Yet, when she noticed the stairs, her adventuresome spirit rekindled her energy and up she went. At the top she found one huge room with three beds. There was an enormous bed that looked so inviting that she tried to pull herself up onto it, but it was far too high. Next she tried the somewhat large bed, which was covered with a beautiful quilt and many plump pillows; however, pull as she might, it too was much too high for her to summit. However, on the opposite side of the room she discovered a small cot covered with the most wonderful, pink blanket one could ever imagine. As she ran her hand across its inviting softness, she decided to just lie down for a minute or two. Alas, she fell sound asleep.

It was then that the three bears came home from their walk. They took one look at the kitchen table and knew they'd had a visitor. "Who's been eating our porridge?" they all shouted.

"And, Baby's porridge is all gone!" exclaimed Baby Bear.

Father Bear ran into the living room with Mama and Baby at his heels. "Oh, my!" cried Mama Bear.

"Someone's been sitting in my chair," they each shouted, echoing each other.

Then, between her tears, Baby Bear sobbed, "Baby's chair. All gone." She continued to cry, so to console her, Papa Bear picked her up. Then, he hugged her and said in a comforting manner, "It's all right. Papa will fix it. Don't cry."

However, considering how his home had been invaded, her father was growing ever so angry. He hurriedly turned to Mama and suggested, "Let's check upstairs." So, the three bears headed for the bedroom.

They dashed into the large room, anxious to discover what was going on. Papa immediately noticed his bed and gruffly grumped, "Someone's been in my bed."

About the same time, Mama also noticed the disheveled quilt and responded, "Someone's been in my bed, too."

Then, a very excited baby bear squealed, "Someone in my bed! Here her is!" All the commotion startled Goldilocks, who jumped up, took one look at those three incredulous bears, and ran from the house as fast as she could. She ran and ran and eventually ran right into the arms of her mother and father, who had decided to search the forest when they could not find their little girl.

The family hugged and kissed and kissed and hugged, they were so happy to see each other. Finally, when the excitement of their reunion began to wane, Goldilocks looked at her parents, and grateful to be rescued, vowed, "I will never, ever go into the forest alone again." And, they believed her.

The Grasshopper and the Ants

Retold by Ardith Davis Cole

"Heave-ho! Heave-ho! Heave-ho!" sang out an army of ants hoisting winter wares upon their wee but mighty shoulders. One after another they marched along, replenishing the cache that would assure their survival over the long, harsh months of ice and snow.

A grasshopper sat alongside their trail, playing casually upon his fiddle. He took little notice of the ants' common mission until an overburdened little fellow tripped over the hopper's outstretched appendage and went tumbling head over heels. Finally coming to a stop, he found that his load had landed right in the lap of the resting grasshopper.

"Sorry," apologized Ant.

"Quite all right, my friend," responded Grasshopper. "Where are you and your friends going with all that food? Is there a party I'm missing? Do they need a fiddler?"

"Oh no, sir," answered Ant, finally recovering from his spill. "We are preparing for winter."

Better Answers

"Winter! Winter? Why, winter is months away! There is plenty of time before winter. Why work so hard when you can play? Look at me. I'm having a wonderful time here in the sun with my fiddle," coaxed Grasshopper.

"Yes, but when the cold winds blow, you may be sorry you did not work harder when the sun was shining," reminded Ant. "I apologize that I cannot stand here and talk, but there is work to be done. Good-bye."

"Good-bye, my little friend," Grasshopper called, as he leaned back to take his afternoon nap.

Months passed, and Grasshopper continued to play while the ants continued to work. Then, one day when Grasshopper arose to play his morning tunes, thick frost lay upon the ground and a cold winter wind pierced his shell.

"Guess I'd better gather some goods for winter," he muttered to himself. "Br-r-r-r. It turned cold fast." Thus, he began his search for food. Whether collected, eaten, or rotted, the abundance of summer was now gone.

"What shall I do?" cried Grasshopper. "I will surely die."

"Help! Help!" he called. "Help!"

Inside the warm and well-supplied trunk of a dead tree, the ants heard Grasshopper's frantic pleas. Together they decided that his was a lesson well learned, and they had more than enough for a very foolish friend, who would no doubt be far wiser when the warm winds once again brought abundance for all who are wise enough to claim it.

The Lion and the Mouse

Retold by Ardith Davis Cole

There was once a fierce and mighty lion who enjoyed catching and tormenting little mice before he ate them. It so happened that as he was walking through the grasslands one day, a little brown mouse scurried by. "BAM!" went his paw, down on the tail of that small, furry creature.

Shaking with fear, the helpless victim squeaked, "Oh, please, kind sir, release me and I will someday return the favor."

"HA!" scoffed the lion. "A wee creature like you help the king of the jungle?" Yet, as the lion sat there listening to his helpless prey beg for his life to be spared, the fierce feline's mood mellowed. He began to consider giving this one mouse his freedom. And so he did.

The sun would set many times before the two of them would meet again. It happened one day as the lion was stalking a small animal on the edge of the great forest. Alas, the fierce beast did not notice the snare that had been set by some hunters, and so he walked directly into it. "SNAP!" went the prison of ropes, capturing the large creature in its grip.

"Help! Help! Help!" roared the mighty beast, caught in the net. Not far away the little mouse heard the lion's call for help, so the tiny creature ran as fast as he could, found the trapped lion, gnawed on the ropes, and freed his friend. As they were about to go their own ways, the mouse turned back and said, "You see, my friend, even those who seem small and insignificant can sometimes help the great and mighty."

The City Mouse and the Country Mouse

Retold by Ardith Davis Cole

A City Mouse and a Country Mouse were acquaintances, so the Country Mouse one day invited his friend to come and see him at his home in the fields. The City Mouse walked and walked until he came to the home of the Country Mouse. A little while after City Mouse had arrived, they sat down to a dinner of barleycorns and roots, which tasted very much like the earth from which they came. The food did not appeal to the guest, and before long he broke out with, "My poor, dear friend, you live here no better than the ants in the ground. Now, you should see how I live! My place overflows with a vast variety of wonderful tastes of every sort. You must come and stay with me, and I promise you, you shall live in the lap of luxury."

So, the next day when the City Mouse returned to town he took the Country Mouse with him and showed him a bountiful quantity of flour and oatmeal and figs and honey and dates. "Indeed, how fortunate you are," exclaimed that Country Mouse, for he had never seen anything like it. So he sat right down to enjoy the plentiful meal his friend provided.

But before they had even begun to eat, they heard footsteps, and then the door of the room opened and someone came in. "Hurry," whispered the City Mouse in a frightened voice. "Hide!" The two mice scampered off and hid themselves in a narrow and exceedingly uncomfortable hole in a far corner of the room. They waited for what seemed like hours. Eventually, when all was quiet, they ventured out again. No sooner had they begun to nibble than someone else came down the hall and opened the door again. Off they scuttled once more.

All of this was too much for the visitor. "Good-bye," said he, "I'm off. You live in the lap of luxury, I can see, but you are surrounded by dangers; whereas at home I can enjoy my simple dinner of roots and corn in peace."

Questions and Petitions Related to Fairy Tales and Fables

For each of the following, use evidence from the story to support your answers.

"Little Red Riding Hood"
> *Task:* How did the wolf fool Little Red Riding Hood?
>
> *Task:* Explain what made Little Red Riding Hood grow suspicious of the wolf when she arrived at Grandmother's.

"The Three Little Pigs"
> *Task:* Why were the houses of Pig 1 and Pig 2 so weak?
>
> *Task:* Describe the personality of each pig.

"Goldilocks and the Three Bears"
> *Task:* Why was the bears' house a mess when they arrived home from their walk?
>
> *Task:* Explain what the bears will have to do now to rectify the antics of Goldilocks.

"The Grasshopper and the Ants"
> *Task:* Why were the ants working so hard in the story?
>
> *Task:* Describe what kind of a character Grasshopper is.

"The Lion and the Mouse"
> *Task:* Why did Mouse help Lion?
>
> *Task:* Why did Lion think Mouse would never be able to help him?

"The City Mouse and the Country Mouse"
> *Task:* Explain why Country Mouse could not live in City Mouse's house.
>
> *Task:* How were the houses of City Mouse and Country Mouse different?

Three Environmental Articles with Questions and Petition Prompts

B

Contents

After a raft of modeling that uses simplistic tales, it is wise to move into high-interest essay texts, such as those in *Chicken Soup for the Soul* (Canfield and Hansen 1993). However, once students have a sound background, you might try modeling from some of the following environmental articles, along with their tasks. Use the Better Answer formula in the same fashion with these more challenging texts as you used with the simpler stories.

The following articles have been reprinted by gracious permission of The Nature Conservancy and the Wilderness Society. One of these articles was taken from the Internet; however, membership in environmental organizations offers a steady stream of such interesting and cause-driven publications. Furthermore, I use the persuasion-oriented letters I receive from these groups to demonstrate exemplary, real-world purposes for writing. Plus, such mindfully constructed persuasive writing serves as a wonderful example for the form and style of a persuasive letter. These exemplary letters can also be found on-line (see Appendix F).

Many environmental organizations have student subgroups, most of whom have their own publications. This provides yet another channel for reading and publishing real-world essays.

One last advantage is that environmental news, essays, and information often align quite nicely with the social studies, science, and health curricula. Therefore, using these publications can only serve to enhance existing texts.

National Monuments *Under Attack*

Only five months ago conservationists and others were celebrating designation of Upper Missouri River Breaks National Monument as a way to protect a stretch of the river in central Montana. But now there are signs that the Bush administration, U.S. Senator Conrad Burns (R-MT), and Congressman Dennis Rehberg (R-MT) are seeking ways to allow coal-bed methane development and oil and gas drilling there. The resulting rigs, roads, buildings, and traffic would pollute the water, destroy archaeological sites, and damage habitat vital to elk, mule deer, and sage grouse, among others.

The Bush administration has said that it does not plan to undo the 22 national monuments created or expanded over the past five years. (In fact, under the Antiquities Act, only Congress has that power.) "But if they attempt to reduce a monument's acreage and then draw up a management plan allowing those destructive activities that the monument was designed expressly to prevent, it amounts to the same thing," says The Wilderness Society's Dave Alberswerth. Across the West, we are working with partners to mobilize public support to block such efforts.

Another threatened monument is Grand Staircase-Escalante in southern Utah. Congressman James Hansen (R-UT), chairman of the House Resources Committee, told the *Deseret News:* "You could easily shrink Grand Staircase. Two-thirds of it is nothing special, just mostly sagebrush." That two-thirds includes the spectacular Kaiparowits Plateau, and its removal from the monument would facilitate massive coal mining. It was that very threat that provided much of the impetus to create this outstanding monument in the first place.

Also facing immediate threats are Ironwood Forest and Sonoran Desert National Monuments, both in southern Arizona. ASARCO, a multinational mining company, has spoken with federal officials about splitting Ironwood Forest into four pieces to accommodate an expanded open-pit copper mine in what is now the heart of the monument. Sonoran may be reduced to permit a power line corridor to slice through the middle of the area and to allow for a car race. Meanwhile, the Bush administration has expressed interest in oil drilling at California's Carrizo Plain National Monument and expansion of commercial fishing at U.S. Virgin Islands Coral Reef National Monument.

"The administration keeps saying that these monuments were established without any effort to hear the views of local residents," says Alberswerth. "That's just not true. Interior Secretary Babbitt spent much of last year crisscrossing the West holding public meetings to find out exactly how people felt."

Current Interior Secretary Gale A. Norton and Congressman Hansen have sent letters to governors, members of Congress, and other politicians inviting them to seek changes in the monuments. "These critics like to overstate the quantity of land protected," says Darrell Knuffke, who directs The Wilderness Society's field staff. "The 22 monuments add up to about six million acres. That's just one percent of the land that belongs to all Americans. That does not strike me as an excessive amount of land to leave in its natural condition."

Please contact Interior Secretary Norton (1849 C St., NW, Washington, DC 20240; 202-208-7351) and your representatives in Congress (Washington, DC 20515 for House and 20510 for Senate; 202-224-3121) to urge them to maintain the level of protection these places currently have.

Reprinted by permission

Roadless Forests:
Death by Poison Pill

Conservationists' efforts to protect 58.5 million acres of roadless national forest land suffered a setback in May when the Bush administration announced that it intends to amend this new national policy forest-by-forest. "The administration sugarcoated this news by saying the policy would stand," says Mike Anderson, Senior Resource Analyst in our Seattle office, "but then indicated that Forest Service officials would be allowed to make exceptions based on local conditions. That's another way of saying that the logging industry will have an opportunity to weaken the policy."

The administration explained its action by maintaining that local interests had not been fully consulted in development of the new rules, which bar road building and most logging in these pristine areas. "The truth," says Anderson, "is that there's never been a federal regulation that was based on so much local input." The Forest Service held 600 hearings around the country and reviewed a record 1.6 million public comments.

In addition to pressing its case with the new administration in Washington, the logging industry has gone to court to challenge the policy. Along with seven other groups in the Heritage Forest Campaign, we have won court approval to be involved in these lawsuits in order to present the reasons for moving forward with this policy.

To step up our long-term campaign to help citizens protect our national forests, we have just created a National Forest Activist Training Institute. The heart of it is a series of day-long workshops around the country to share knowledge on how to communicate with the media, conduct research, and mobilize grassroots support, among other subjects.

More than half of the acreage in the national forests has been roaded or otherwise developed, and we believe the one-third of the forest system that is roadless—but currently not protected as wilderness areas—needs to be left just as it is. The benefits of doing so include cleaner air and water, viable habitat for fish and wildlife that need undisturbed areas, recreation opportunities, and the local economic boost that these natural areas provide by luring visitors. The national forests already contain about 400,000 miles of roads, enough to circle the planet 16 times.

You can help defend these roadless areas by urging U.S. Forest Service Chief Dale Bosworth not to amend the rule. (201 14th St., SW, Washington, DC 20090; 202-205-1661)

More information:
www.wilderness.org/roadless.htm

Visit a Place Near You:
Where We Work

Search: (Tips)
(a)

Bioreserves

Kentucky

Kentucky Home
About the Chapter
Places We Protect
Bioreserves
How You Can Help
Volunteer Opportunities
Events
Slide Shows
Chapter News
Contact Us
Related Links

© Richie Kessler

River Speak

By Richie Kessler

We often talk about how nature speaks to us. Nature may speak to us in many different ways it excites us, calms us, motivates us, wraps us in serenity, or even scares us. It probably speaks to each of us in different ways in this sense, nature is multilingual! I often have wondered if Green River could speak to us, what would it say? And how would we refer to Green River? Is the Green River an it, a he (like old man river), or a she? For now, I believe I will pay it the proper respect and refer to the Green as a "she".

I am sure if she could talk she could tell us how for millennia she has cut through the valley, creating new channels, rediscovering old ones, and making habitats all the time. Similarly, she could describe for us how, as she cut the valley, she also contributed to the formation of the world's largest cave system. Maybe she would tell us of how the most recent period of glaciation, several thousands of years ago, stopped just short of her doorstep, sparing her landscape and topography from eternal alteration and enhancing her potential for the great biological diversity found in her waters even today.

More recently, she might recall how early native Americans fished her waters or sought shelter in her caves. Or how our ancestors shipped supplies down the Green to the Ohio, Mississippi and beyond. She might remember the echo of gunfire as Union and Confederate soldiers battled for positions along its length including sites like Tebb's Bend and Munfordville, or the echo of a Kentucky rifle as a great-great grandfather harvested a squirrel from an overhanging sycamore limb. Maybe she would describe for us how our predecessors used to visit town by crossing her spine on a cable ferry at Greensburg.

She laughingly remembers having her ribs of Brush Creek, Little Barren, Lynn Camp Creek and Russell Creek tickled by the splashing feet of the youth of yesterday. However, she won't hesitate to remind you that, in combination with her tributaries and in spite of efforts to control her, she can become a powerful force worthy of our respect in a matter of minutes. She has caused communities like Greensburg to tremble at her rising waters more than once in history. Her strong pulses have put life into our valleys by richening our soils for agriculture. Her force has powered the production of grist mills like the Montgomery Mill on Pitman Creek and Three Hundred Springs Mill on Green River. Even though she supports and sustains our life, she also is powerful enough to take it away.

As a mother proudly boasts of her children, she would also want us to know that she is home to the greatest fish and mussel diversity of any river system in Kentucky. From Green River dam to Mammoth Cave, she is home to 109 types of fishes and nearly 60 different kinds of mussels, many of them exceedingly rare. And you ought to see her basement! Her underground streams contain some of the most unique and rare organisms on earth. Indeed, if she were considered a house and her rooms habitats, she would be one of the freshwater mansions of North America. A Biltmore estate of freshwater diversity! We are fortunate to have so much to care about—so much to conserve.

As impressive as this sounds, however, she might also complain a little. She has earned the right after all. She might relay to us how she has become "stressed out" in recent times as our populations have grown along with our demands on the lands that border her. She would tell us how we have littered her once beautiful cliffs with rubber tires, water heaters, or other modern "throw away" items. Or how we have polluted her waters in a myriad of ways and altered her flow and temperatures. Many of her fishes (~%) and mussels (%) are imperiled, meaning the future is not secure. I guess we could say she is a freshwater mansion in need of some repair. Indeed, nearly seventy miles of her two banks and bottoms are in need of some form of restoration.

Green River would also tell us that she is resilient. Despite the stresses of mankind, upper Green River continues to support an amazing number of fish and wildlife species and a number of human uses. We must remember, throughout its history, this river has sustained itself with or without man (or due to his absence). Alternatively, man has depended on its waters and will continue to do so throughout his existence.

Interestingly, although people have altered the river and threaten it in many ways, it is also people who have the ability to protect the river for future generations. Once, sections of Pitman Creek near Campbellsville were practically devoid of fish life due to pollution by dies and heavy metals from a local industry. When this stress was reduced and, eventually removed, many species of fishes returned. Through the efforts of many, an underground stream at Horse Cave once regarded as an open sewer now is home to a museum. The site is now a popular tourist attraction where visitors can see aquatic cave life prospering once again. Around 1960 the oil boom in Green, Hart, and Metcalfe counties resulted in petroleum and brine being flushed into many streams. Some of the small streams were virtually killed out. The effects of runoff from Green County were felt all the way to Mammoth Cave. Many of these streams, thankfully, have recovered to some degree.

Even though she is resilient, it is hard to predict the ultimate effect of these cumulative stresses not only on the fish and wildlife but also on the water quality, which affects us all. I interpret her message to be that if given a fair chance she will continue to provide us the various benefits we have come to expect and perhaps have taken for granted, in the past.

Okay, so the Green River doesn't really speak. Maybe she actually depends on us to speak for her. Yes, her people are her voice. But imagine for a minute if she could speak, would anyone listen?

Back to Bioreserves

Reprinted by permission

Questions and Petitions Related to Environmental Articles

"National Monuments Under Attack," *The Wilderness Society Newsletter,* Summer 2001, Vol. III: 3.

> *Task:* How are our national monuments being threatened? Use evidence from the article to support your answer.

> *Task:* How do those encroaching on national monuments justify their actions? Use evidence from the article to support your answer.

"Roadless Forests: Death by Poison Pill," *The Wilderness Society Newsletter,* Summer 2001, Vol. III: 3.

> *Task:* What actions are being taken to protect our national forests? Use the article to support your answer.

> *Task:* Why does this author think road-building in the national forests is unnecessary? Support your answer with details from the article.

Kessier, R. 2001. Kentucky: Bioreserves: "River Speak." www.tnc.org/

> *Task:* Why is it important to protect plants and animals from extinction? Use the article to explain your answer.

> *Task:* How might the future be different if we were to lose rose periwinkle, crabs, and the desert creosote bush? Use the article to explain your answer.

Samples of Students' Responses

The following section contains many different examples of students' responses to prompts developed from two fables (see Appendix A for the versions of the fables used for this activity). I tried to collect pieces from students who were performing at a variety of levels to provide your students with multiple and varied assessment opportunities. Students become fascinated in the progress of others, and because these responses belong to strangers they feel free to assess and offer suggestions for how each product could be improved. Assessment of others' responses will help students assess their own writing.

There is no one right answer related to how each of these students could be helped, or for that matter, what exactly is wrong or right with each piece. They just serve as evaluation grist, a common source that can be copied onto a transparency or individual papers for observation and discussion. I intended that these would be made into transparencies to "save a tree"; however, if they are copied onto paper for each student, please save and reuse the copies from year to year. The common viewing and reference that transparencies allow, however, makes them a far better tool.

The Better Answer scale should be in full view as each of these pieces is discussed. Furthermore, it helps to use them throughout the various steps, rather than waiting until the journey is complete. Accordingly, as your class works with restating the question, search out a good example of a student who did and another who did not restate; then, use those examples to undergird the concept. In that way, the examples here will eventually become anchors for future reference.

You will notice that the following prompts and set of responses relate to "The Lion and the Mouse" fable. Before students evaluate these samples, they should, of course, have heard or read that story. The same applies to the second set of responses and their prompt, which relate to "The City Mouse and the Country Mouse."

Students' Responses to "The Lion and the Mouse" Prompt

Why did the little mouse say "Even those who seem small and insignificant can sometimes help the great and mighty"? Be sure to include details from the story in your answer.

1

> Mouse said even those who seem small and insignificant can sometimes help the great and mighty because he wanted the lion to know he was just as big as the lion. He set that big lion free and so he was just as him. That is why he said even those who seem small and insignificant can sometimes help the great and mighty.

2

> Yes because mouse is not insignificant because he helped lion out of the net. He is significant. That is why.

3

Mouse said that because he is not small and he proved it!

4

Lion caut mouse and mouse asked him to let go so then when lion was caut mouse helped him too, That is why he said that.

5

There was once a mouse Dipt by a lion. He was frayed so the lion let him go. Then one day he repad the lion by helping him get loos out of the hunter's roops He chood on them an the lion got away. He was a brave mouse.

6

Mouse said, "Even those who seem small and insignificant can sometimes help the great and mighty." because he wanted the lion to see that even though he was little he could repay a big lion who did him a favor. When mouse got caught by lion and asked lion to let him go and he would someday repay him him the lion did not think mouse could ever repay, but he still gave him his freedom. Then one day when the lion got caught in a hunter's net, the little mouse heard his roars and nawed on the net to set the lion free. That is why the mouse felt he could help even a strong, fierce lion.

7

The little mouse said,"Even those who seem small and insignificant can sometimes help the great and mighty." because when the lion had the mouse trapped, lion said he could not understand how a wee creature like a mouse could help a mighty lion. Lion said this because the mouse was begging for his life. The king of the jungle did set the mouse free. Therefore, one day whe. the lion get caught in a net set by some hunters, the mouse heard his cries for help. So that little creature ran and gnawed the ropes and set the lion free. Mouse might be small but he still showed that he was mighty. That is why the mouse said, "Even those who seem small and insignificant can sometimes help the great and mighty".

8

He said that because he wanted lion to know that he could help him when he needed help because lion helped him and he would always be his friend.

9

The little mouse said that because he wanted to tell the lion that no matter how small or little you are, you can still be brave and help others. You can always help others big and brave, or small and shy. Just because the big can help the little, doesn't mean the little can't help the big.

10

The mouse said that because, even though the mouse
~~he was~~ smaller ^than^ ~~the.~~ ^lion^ ~~he~~ was, he could still
do anything ^the lion^ ~~the~~ could. He might not be
to insignificant, he can at least save a
life. He might not be great and mighty,
be he is brave, and keeps his promises.
Although, the mouse isn't all that I said
to some people, but to me he is a very
insignificant, brave, great, and mighty mouse.

11

Most people think that a mouse
can not help a lion, but they
are wrong because in this story
a mouse does help a lion.
He gnaws the rope and lets
the lion go. That is why it
said even those who seem
small and insignificant can
sometimes help the great and
mighty

Students' Responses to "The City Mouse and the Country Mouse" Prompt

Why did the Country Mouse decide to go back home? Be sure to include details from the story in your answer.

1

> Because it was too danger in the city. And that not his kind of home. He like the country Because it paeceful He like corn and root. I like the part when the country mouse Go home Because the city is not his Kind of home. I think the country should live in the country. And the city mouse should live in the City

2

> The Country Mouse was tramandsly scared. The Country mouse said: " You live in danger." The Cuntry mouse and the City Mouse ate corn and something else.

3

> The country Mouse decided to go home because Somone came in the City Mouses house and said You May live in a wonderful house but their's danger all around. The country mouse probbly didn't want to get eaten. I know if I were him I wouldn't want to get eaten. Especially by a cat. And that's why he probably went home.

The country mouse decided to go back home because
the city mouse lived in the house of
Dangurel. And if the city mouse
lived in the house they would probly
be poisned or be snaped with a mouse
trap and then they be dead for
ever I love mice, ginepigs, hamsters
I love all kinds of anmals and I
don't want them to die I fell sosorry
for all those dead anmals and
the most anmal I love is cats, and
dogs. But the barking dogs the mean
cats and dogs. The country mouse
should have left with the city mouse
iF he hadn't he would have been dead.

5

The contry mouse decided to go back. because
they hard footprance and they got in a little hool
than they got out and the cointry mouse
sade to the city mouse that the city mouse
lives in danger, and the country mouse sade et
homme he cut eat flower and corn at silonte.
so he disided to leave the city mouses homme.
and wen he sade that he is leaveng he
want it so he left the city mouse left

The country mouse sid this is not a good place, because
it is veay loud sound and in the country it is not no
sound. the two mouse got out of the couner the door open
and the two mouse got up and the country mouse said
the coustry is quilt and I am going to the coustry because
it is quiet.

7

The country mouse dicided to go back home becausse he said," I can enjoy a meal at home without anybody eteruping me." So the country mouse went home to eat. The country mouse wanted to go home because the city was too dangrous for him. But the city mouse was use to it and the country mouse wasn't use to it. So he thout he might be better at his own house. And he though that the city mouse would be better at his own house to. The country mouse dicided to go to the city because the city mouse came to his house so he went to the city. The city mouse and the country mouse went to each others house and saw what it was like to live in the city and in the country.

8

The country mouse decided to go back home because he thought that the city mouse lived around danger and that having dinner there would not be peaceful. The country mouse didn't want to stay because he thought that it would not be safe. He said that he would go home and have dinner by him self then nobody would bother him. the country mouse would not be happy in the city.

9

The Country Mouse decided to go home because he did not feel comfortable there. He though it was to dangerous. I think the City Mouse felt bad when the Country Mouse left. The Country Mouse was happy to have a friend over his house but his friend was not very polite. The City Mouse did not like the food that the Coutry Mouse made, and he said that the Coutry Mouse lived no better than an ant. That was not very nice. "I dont think the Coutry Mouse had much fun in the City." I think the Country Mouse was happy when he was home. The City Mouse lives in the city and the Country Mouse lives in the country. They both have different homes and they both are different from eachother.

10

The, Country mouse, decided to go home because there it was to cat a dangrouse cat that loves to eat mice. The country mouse invited City mouse and his friends. city mouse said to country mouse come to my home. and then when Country mouse saw Cities mouse house city mouse said look at the flowers and oat meal. I think country mouse started getting jalous.

11

The country mouse wanted too go back home because he knew it was dangerous too live in a place where you could get caught by any one! So he said I've got too go home! And he went home and ate hes roots and corn!

12

Because they kept trying to get food but they kept hearing foot steps. So he decide to go home because he could not get Honey or frash roots. When the country mouse went to the city he was happy because he did not want to eat old roots. But when the country mouse want to the city he kept trying to get food but he could not get food so he want back to the country.

13

The country Mouse decided to go back to the country of because she know that the city mouse was in danger. She said I'll rather go to the country and live like a ant under ground like you told me when you came to the country.

Lesson Plans for the Better Answer Formula

D

Contents

The following lesson plans were written using real lessons that worked. They are included for your convenience; however, please feel free to rework them in a manner that might better suit your own purposes.

Each of the five Better Answer steps has a lesson introductory plan that is grounded in teacher modeling. To illustrate, I include lesson plans for some of these. Then a second lesson is included for each step as a natural follow-up. It therefore involves guided participation; that is, the students will be trying on the protocol for size, but the teacher is still supporting and scaffolding them. Each step evolves through the same instructional sequence, from a time when the teacher is completely demonstrating the task continuing on through a gradual kind of weaning as students have more and more independence and the teacher plays less and less of a part. In the end, it's all theirs.

Topic: Restating a Question

Scaffolding Level: Initial modeling

Goal: Students will observe and minimally participate as teacher demonstrates how to restate a question.

Materials: several pieces of large, blank chart paper on an easel or taped to the wall; list of known-answer questions (see below) spaced on laminated chart; erasable marker

Known-Answer Questions
1. What did you do last night when you got home from school?
2. How do you and your family have fun together?
3. Why should all children have the privilege of attending school?
4. How does school help prepare you for the job you will someday have?
5. How would you change our school, if it were possible?

Procedure
Part 1: Explain why we want to restate the question (to look good, sound smart, and get off to a good start). Mention National Public Radio interviews!

Part 2: Use the first chart question to show how to mark a question during or after restating it. Also write a restatement of the question below it. An example follows.

What did you do <u>last</u> <u>night</u> <u>when</u> ~~you~~ <u>got</u> <u>home</u> <u>from</u> <u>school</u>?
Last night when I got home from school I . . .
(Leave space for answer in Step 2.)

Part 3: Explain open-ended restatements that temporarily end with an ellipsis, which will be erased when we get to Step 2.
Part 4: Model Question 2 on the chart in the same manner, but invite one student to mark the question and another to scribe the restatement as it is dictated.

104

Part 5: Model the rest of the sentences in the same fashion, inviting two students each time to replicate Part 4 tasks. After each sentence is done, ask if anyone else sees another way it can be restated. Honor these by writing them on the board for observation.

Closure
Part 6: Ask class to watch throughout the day for written questions that can be restated. We'll share some before we leave.

Topic: Restating a Question

Scaffolding Level: Guided participation

Goal: Partnered students will work together to restate and mark sentences, which will later be used during whole-class community share.

Materials: One copy of known-answer questions for each student; a large chart with spaced question list (or transparency of the same); marker

Known-Answer Questions
1. Why is it important to be on time for school and other events?
2. Why is it a good thing to work with another person on a school project?
3. Why is it important to complete homework each day?
4. How might math be helpful to you when you are not in school?
5. What would you do to help a forgetful friend to remember his or her homework every day?

Procedure
Part 1: Return to the restatement chart (from Lesson 1-A). Review.

Part 2: Pass out copies of questions to partnered students. Explain the task (to mark questions transformed into restatements) and remind students that we will have community share in about 15 minutes.

Part 3: Cruise the room, scaffolding students as they work on restatements.

Closure
Part 4: As community shares, use the chart (or transparency) to scribe responses. Save for Lesson 2-B. Collect student papers also to use for Lesson 2-B.

Topic: Constructing a General, or Gist, Answer

Scaffolding Level: Modeling

Goal: Students will observe how to construct a general, or gist, answer after a restatement of a question.

Materials: Original question charts (from Lesson 1-A) with their restatements; marker

Procedure

Part 1: Explain general, or gist, answers. They are answers that include no details and make us want to ask, "What do you mean?"

Part 2: Use Question 1 to demonstrate. Provide several examples.

What did you do <u>last</u> <u>night</u> <u>when</u> ~~you~~ <u>got</u> <u>home</u> <u>from</u> <u>school</u>?
Last night when I got home from school I . . .

    —had fun.   —played with my friends.
    —was bored.   —had to work really hard.
    —had a problem.   —had to go visiting.

Part 3: Show how each answer begs the question, "What do you mean?" which would then call for details to explain that answer. BUT no details will be added yet (that's Step 3).

Part 4: Select one answer that applies to the teacher, and transfer it to finish a restatement on original chart. It should then serve as an example of a restatement with an attached gist answer.

Part 5: Use Question 2 to demonstrate.

Part 6: Invite students to come forward to eliminate the ellipsis for each restatement of questions on the original chart and then scribe a gist answer as the class works together with teacher to create gist answers for Questions 3 through 5.

Closure

Part 7: Use a text question, inviting class to restate and answer with only a gist answer.

Topic: Constructing a General, or Gist, Answer

Scaffolding Level: Guided participation

Goal: Dyads will work together to construct a gist answer using their previous restated (known-answer) questions.

Materials: Lesson 1-B questions with restatements returned to original owners; marker

Procedure

Part 1: Return to Lesson 2-A chart to review gist answers.

Part 2: Invite dyads to work together constructing a gist answer for first restatement. Cruise the room, scaffolding students toward success. When most appear finished, call attention for whole-group share.

Part 3: Invite dyads to continue constructing gist answers for Questions 3 through 5. Cruise the room, scaffolding.

Closure

Part 4: Whole-group share: Use students' responses to complete the group charted questions from Lesson 1-B. Post them on the wall as a permanent example (an anchor).

Topic: "The Answer Sandwich" with the Answer Organizer Framework

Scaffolding Level: Modeling

Goal: Students will observe how to use the Answer Organizer framework to develop an answer for a question from "Little Red Riding Hood."

Materials: Wall chart containing list of midparagraph transition terms; blank chart paper; Answer Organizer framework chart and Answer Sandwich chart posted; marker; transparency or chart with following question: How did Little Red Riding Hood know that the character in the bed was not her grandmother?; brief version of "Little Red Riding Hood."

Procedure

Part 1: Review the Answer Sandwich chart. Explain that today's focus will involve the use of the Answer Organizer (show chart) to log separate answer sections.

Part 2: Post question from "Little Red Riding Hood." Read question, then the story.

Part 3: Reread question: How did Little Red Riding Hood know that the character in the bed was not her grandmother? On the Answer Organizer chart scribe restatement as a class member restates. Use right-hand column, across from "Restatement" in left column, to write restatement.

Part 4: Discuss a gist answer with the group. Scribe a gist answer into right column of the Answer Organizer chart in proper place.

Part 5: Review some of the details that could help support the gist answer. As this is done, jot each onto the blank chart paper. Afterward, discuss with the class how chronological order will be used to log each detail onto the middle section of the sandwich; however, terms from "Transitions" wall chart will also be accessed to help the entire piece "flow together and sound connected."

Part 6: Using transition terms to connect pieces, scribe sentences with details into right column on the Answer Organizer chart in their proper placement. Reread whole "to see if it sounds right."

Part 7: Remind students that this is a time we can use "This is how" from the bottom of the sandwich. Write this phrase across from "Concluding Statement" on the Answer Organizer chart. Next demonstrate how we merely return to the restatement to bring closure to our Answer Sandwich construction and complete the remainder of "This is how . . ."

Part 8: Ask students to investigate other possible concluding statements. Scribe on board as they are dictated.

Closure

Part 9: Call for a student to read "Little Red Riding Hood" question, and another to read the entire answer that we have constructed. Suggest that they use this form when they are answering questions in math, science, social studies, and other areas of the curriculum. Post permanently so all can use as an "anchor."

Topic: "The Answer Sandwich" with the Answer Organizer Framework

Scaffolding Level: Guided participation

Goal: Students will practice using the Answer Organizer framework to develop an answer for question from "Goldilocks and the Three Bears."

Materials: Wall chart containing list of midparagraph transition terms; copies of the Answer Organizer for each student; Answer Sandwich chart posted; marker; transparency or chart with following question: Why were the three bears so upset when they got home from their walk?; brief version of "Goldilocks and the Three Bears."

Procedure

Part 1: Review the Answer Organizer framework from "Little Red Riding Hood" question.

Part 2: Post question from "Goldilocks and the Three Bears." Read question, then the story.

Part 3: Reread question: Why were the three bears so upset when they got home from their walk?

Part 4: Pass out copies of the Answer Organizer framework to each student. Partner students to collaboratively construct an answer to the question using the Answer Organizer framework. Cruise the room, scaffolding as students work.

Part 5: In a whole-class community, invite students to share parts as teacher scribes *all* answer parts onto chart paper.

Closure

Part 6: Draw students' attention to the fact that although most students answered in a different manner, most were still correct—as long as they carefully followed the Answer Sandwich protocol and carefully included details to support their answers. Post examples on wall for future reference.

Topic: Conferring after Answering Test Questions

Scaffolding Level: Individual teacher-student conference

Goal: Using the Better Answer scale in a teacher conference situation, students will (1) understand their strengths in answering questions, but they will (2) also be able to articulate one area for improvement during their next question-answering experience. (Order of importance on scale is from the top downward. That is, if the student cannot develop a gist answer, we should not focus him on conventions. Content first!)

Materials: Extended-response or essay answers (from a current test), which have been evaluated for alignment with the Better Answer scale; Better Answer scale marked and stapled to each response

Procedure

Part 1: Explain that students will be called aside in order to survey the way in which their recent test answers align with the Better Answer formula, while other students will be working on a project or assignment.

Part 2: Call students aside one at a time. Using their test questions, which have been evaluated for alignment, draw attention first to noticeable strengths. Afterward, focus on one area in which they need to improve. Discuss a strategy for improvement. Before exiting, each student should respond to the following question: The next time you answer a written question, what will your focus be?

Closure

Part 3: After all students have had an alignment conference, ask them to share with a partner what their goal will be the next time they have to answer a written question, as well as the strategy that will move them to success.

Spreadsheets to Monitor Answer Performance

This section is included to provide an easy means of tracking individual student and class response performance. Basically, this appendix shows two kinds of spreadsheets for collecting data, one that can be used to follow the progress of individual students and one that can provide an at-a-glance summary of the status of the entire class.

An actual page from a whole-class data sample has also been included to provide an example of what that might look like. These samples were baseline data collected *before* students received instruction using the Better Answer formula. I did change the names of these students; and, because more than half of them were ESL, I substituted similar multicultural names.

It is easy to see how helpful these spreadsheets might be when the teacher meets with a parent in search of a way to help, when child study teams meet, or when students, themselves, need to see their own progress on paper. Additionally, a whole-class spreadsheet can be a very quick way to decide which students should be invited into any given mini-lesson. And the best part is that it takes very little time to log the information.

The Better Answer Scale

Name _____ Date _____

	Minimally 1	Partially 2	Completely 3
Restates question in the answer	_____	_____	_____
Develops a gist answer	_____	_____	_____
Uses details from text to support the answer	_____	_____	_____
Develops conclusion	_____	_____	_____
Stays on topic	_____	_____	_____
Writes very neatly	_____	_____	_____
Uses proper conventions	_____	_____	_____

The Better Answer Scale

Name _____ Date _____

	Minimally 1	Partially 2	Completely 3
Restates question in the answer	_____	_____	_____
Develops a gist answer	_____	_____	_____
Uses details from text to support the answer	_____	_____	_____
Develops conclusion	_____	_____	_____
Stays on topic	_____	_____	_____
Writes very neatly	_____	_____	_____
Uses proper conventions	_____	_____	_____

The Better Answer Scale

Name _____ Date _____

	Minimally 1	Partially 2	Completely 3
Restates question in the answer	_____	_____	_____
Develops a gist answer	_____	_____	_____
Uses details from text to support the answer	_____	_____	_____
Develops conclusion	_____	_____	_____
Stays on topic	_____	_____	_____
Writes very neatly	_____	_____	_____
Uses proper conventions	_____	_____	_____

The Better Answer Scale

Name _____ Date _____

	Minimally 1	Partially 2	Completely 3
Restates question in the answer	_____	_____	_____
Develops a gist answer	_____	_____	_____
Uses details from text to support the answer	_____	_____	_____
Develops conclusion	_____	_____	_____
Stays on topic	_____	_____	_____
Writes very neatly	_____	_____	_____
Uses proper conventions	_____	_____	_____

Monitoring Answer Performance of Individual Students

Student Name _____

Task or Test	Date	Answer Content						Answer Readableness		
		Restates	Gist Answer	Details as Evidence	Develops conclusion	Stays on Topic	Content Total Score	Hand-writing	Conven-tions	Readable-ness Total Score

Monitoring Answer Performance of Total Class

Task or Test _____   Date _____

Students' Names	Room	Answer Content						Answer Readableness		
		Restates	Gist Answer	Details as Evidence	Develops conclusion	Stays on Topic	*Content Total Score*	Hand-writing	Conven-tions	*Readable-ness Total Score*

Monitoring Answer Performance Base-Level Sample from Grade 3 Class
(before implementation of Better Answers)

Task or Test ___"The City Mouse and the Country Mouse"___ Date _____

Students' Names	Room	Answer Content					Answer Readableness		
		Restates	Gist Answer	Details as Evidence	Stays on Topic	Content Total Score	Hand-writing	Conven-tions	Readable-ness Total Score
Andrew	5	1	1	2	1	1	2	2	2
Carmelita	5	1	3	2	2	2	2	2	2
Mohab	5	1	1	2	1	1	1	2	2
Beline	5	1	3	2	2	2	2	1	1
Steve	5	0	0	0	0	0	0	0	0
Delanie	5	2	2	1	2	2	2	2	2
Keoh	5	1	1	1	1	1	2	1	1
Amanda	5	1	1	1	1	1	3	3	3
Tai	5	3	3	2	2	2	2	1	1
Roomel	5	3	3	2	1	2	3	2	2
Julia	5	3	3	2	2	2	1	1	1
Michael	5	3	3	3	3	3	1	2	2
Francis	5	1	2	1	2	2	3	2	2
Nutando	5	3	3	3	2	3	3	1	2
Shiasta	5	1	1	1	1	1	1	1	1
Tiando	5	3	3	2	2	2	1	2	2
Mavis	5	1	1	2	1	1	2	1	2
Ryad	5	2	2	3	2	2	3	2	2
Layla	5	2	2	2	2	2	3	2	2

Resources for Essays and Articles

This section has been developed to provide a raft of background related to locating good essays; however, it seemed important to explain just exactly what an essay is before investigating their sources.

Essay writing falls somewhere between creative writing and expository writing, presenting facts and evidence, but doing so in a narrative style. It's inherently nonfiction, yet shaded with interpretations. Essays can be in article or report form, but according to *Webster's New World Dictionary* (Neufeldt 1991, p. 78) each must be a complete piece of writing. The tone, although often serious, can also be "relaxed and frequently humorous" (*Concise Columbia Encyclopedia* 1994, p. 202). It is that tone that hues the piece with voice, and it is the expectations of the audience that define the tone.

Furthermore, an essay is "expressive of the author's outlook and personality" (Neufeldt 1991, p. 464), and for that reason, point-of-view can subtly, as well as flamboyantly, shade the meaning inherent in the writing. There is nowhere that I know of that this can be more readily experienced than on National Public Radio (NPR), where short essays are read regularly and, depending on the author, reflect this side or that of an issue. NPR listeners seem to enjoy heavy bias; whereas, those correcting examination papers may not. Students need to know this. They need to investigate the essay's grand number of forms. This bibliography will provide an entry point for such a journey.

Resources for Essays and Articles for Grades 3–8

Allenbaugh, K. 2000. *Chocolate for a Teen's Soul: Life-Changing Stories for Young Women About Growing Wise and Growing Strong.* New York: Simon & Schuster.

Baxter, K. A., and M. A. Kochel. 1999. *Gotcha!* Englewood, CO: Libraries Unlimited.

Canfield, J., ed. 1998. *Chicken Soup for the Kid's Soul.* New York: Scholastic. (Written by kids)

Canfield, J. *Chicken Soup for the Soul Collection: Sports Fans, Pets, Dogs, Preteens, Teens . . .* New York: Scholastic.

Carlson, R. 2000. *Don't Sweat the Small Stuff.* New York: Hyperion.

Covey, S. 1998. *Seven Habits of Highly Effective Teens.* New York: Fireside.

Drew, B. A. 1997. *100 Most Popular Young Adult Authors: Biographical Sketches . . .* Englewood, CO: Libraries Unlimited.

Duey, K., and M. Barnes. 2000. *Freaky Facts.* New York: Aladdin.

Editors of Canari Press. *Random Acts of Kindness; More Random Acts of Kindness; Random Acts of Kindness for Kids.* Berkeley, CA: Canari Press.

Haven, K. 1995. *Amazing American Women: 40 Fascinating 5-Minute Reads.* Englewood, CO: Libraries Unlimited.

———. 1998. *Close Encounters with Deadly Dangers: Riveting Reads and Classroom Ideas.* Englewood, CO: Libraries Unlimited.

Haven, K., and D. Clark. 1999. *100 Most Popular Scientists for Young Adults: Biographical Sketches . . .* Englewood, CO: Libraries Unlimited.

Jaffe, Azriela, ed. 2001. *Heart Warmers of Love.* Holbrook, MA: Adams Media.

LaFontaine, P. 2000. *Companions in Courage.* New York: Warner Books.

Meyer, S. H., and J. Meyer. 2000. *Teen Ink.* Deerfield Beach, FL: Health Communications. (Written by teens)

McElmeel, S. L. 1998. *100 Most Popular Children's Authors: Biographical Sketches . . .* Englewood, CO: Libraries Unlimited.

———. 2000. *100 Most Popular Picture Book Authors and Illustrators: Biographical Sketches . . .* Englewood, CO: Libraries Unlimited.

Mendoza, P. M. 1999. *Extraordinary People in Extraordinary Times: Heroes, Sheroes, and Villains.* Englewood, CO: Libraries Unlimited.

Nelson, P. 1993. *Magic Minutes.* Englewood, CO: Libraries Unlimited.

Portalupi, J., and R. Fletcher. 2001. *Nonfiction Craft Lessons: Teaching Information Writing K–8.* Portland, ME: Stenhouse. (In the appendix)

Sark. *Inspiration Sandwich.* Berkeley, CA: Celestial Arts.

Williams, T. 2001. *Stay Strong: Simple Life Lessons for Teens.* New York: Scholastic.

Wyatt, F. R., et al. 1998. *Popular Nonfiction Authors for Children.* Englewood, CO: Libraries Unlimited.

Series Books with Essays for Grades 3–8

Extraordinary Americans Series: (readability 3–4) J. W. Walch
    (www.walch.com):
       16 Extraordinary American Women
       16 Extraordinary Asian Americans
       16 Extraordinary Hispanic Americans
       16 Extraordinary Native Americans
       16 Extraordinary Young Americans
Walch Super Readers: (readability 3–4) J. W. Walch (www.wallch.com):
       Amazing Rescues
       Baffling Disappearances
       Creepy Creatures
       Daring Escapes
       Great Crime Busters
       Great Disasters
       Mysterious Places
       Scary Tales
       Stories of the Presidents
       Unbelievable Beasts
       Unlikely Heroes

High-Interest Authentic Essays/Articles/Reviews on the Web

www.news@envirocitizen.org/news/ (National Environmental Wire for Students)
www.amazon.com/ (Amazon web site has hundreds of book reviews.)
www.bn.com/ (Barnes & Noble web site has hundreds of book reviews.)
www.sierraclub.org/ (Sierra Club is tops for environmental information.)
www.NPR.org/ (National Public Radio is overflowing with short pieces of writing
    and audios.)
www.PBS.org/ (Public Broadcasting System has a bounty of short, current pieces
    of writing and audios.)
www.chinaberry.com/ (those wonderful *Chinaberry* reviews and more on-line)
www.heartwarmers4U.com/ (real-life tales of courage and faith)
www.tnc.org/ (sponsored by The Nature Conservancy with lots of good articles)
www.timeforkids.com (*Time Magazine* for grades 4–7)
www.cobblestonepub.com (articles, essays, lesson plans, and more from
    Cobblestone Publishing Company)
www.discovery.com (AT&T and The Discovery Channel site)
www.thinkquest.org/ (ThinkQuest is a global network of students, teachers, parents,
    and technologists dedicated to exploring youth-centered learning on the Net.)
www.pages.prodigy.com/childrens_writers/ (articles about and by children's authors)
www.carolhurst.com/ (reviews and lessons plans for great kids' books)
www.www.cbs.sportsline.com/u/football/nfl/kids/ (click News for interesting arti-
    cles related to sports)

www.nrich.maths.org.uk/ (click Articles and search for some that challenge those gifted minds)

www.pitara.com/magazine/features.asp (a wonderful web site and magazine from India with many great articles/essays by kids)

www.kidshealth.org/ (the latest on everything from chicken pox to dyslexia in easy-to-read articles for kids, teens, and parents)

www.enn.com/news/enn-stories (The Environmental News Network with daily updates on a variety of issues)

Cooper, G., and C. Cooper. 2001. *New Virtual Field Trips.* Englewood, CO: Libraries Unlimited. (contains a gazillion web sites with short pieces related to every curricular area)

Magazines with Essays and Articles for Grades 3–8

(Most of these magazines also have a web site.)

American Careers, Career Communications, Inc., 6701 W. 64th St., Suite 304, Overland Park, KS 66202.

Byline, P.O. Box 130596, Edmond, OK 73013.

Calliope: Exploring World History, Cobblestone Publishing, Inc., 30 Grove St., Peterborough, NH 03458.

Canada and the World, R/L Taylor Consultants Publishing, P.O. Box 7004, Oakville, ON, Canada L6J6L5.

Child Life, Children's Better Health Institute, P.O. Box 7468, Red Oak, IA 51591.

Children's Digest, Children's Better Health Institute, P.O. Box 7468, Red Oak, IA 51591.

Cicada, Carus Publishing Co., P.O. Box 7705, Red Oak, IA 51591-0705.

Cobblestone, Cobblestone Publishing, Inc., 30 Grove St., Peterborough, NH 03458.

Colorado Kids, The Denver Post, 1560 Broadway, Denver, CO 80202.

7, Prufrock Press, P.O. Box 8813, Waco, TX 76714.

Cricket, Carus Publishing, 315 Fifth St., P.O. Box 300, Peru, IL 61354.

Current Events, Weekly Reader Corp., P.O. Box 2791, Middletown, CN 06457.

Current Science, Weekly Reader Corp., P.O. Box 2791, Middletown, CN 06457.

Dolphin Log, The Cousteau Society, 870 Greenbrier Circle, Suite 402, Chesapeake, VA 23320.

Dragonfly, National Science Teachers Association, 1840 Wilson Boulevard, Arlington, VA 22201.

Faces, Cobblestone Publishing, Inc., 30 Grove St., Peterborough, NH 03458.

Footsteps, Cobblestone Publishing, Inc., 30 Grove St., Peterborough, NH 03458.

Hit Parader, 63 Grand Ave. #200, River Edge, NJ 07661.

Hot Dog Magazine, Scholastic, Inc., 555 Broadway, New York, NY 10012.

How on Earth, Vegetarian Education Network, P.O. Box 3347, West Chester, PA 19381.

Junior Scholastic, Scholastic, Inc., 2931 E. McCarty St., P.O. Box 3710, Jefferson City, MO 65102.

Kids Discover, P.O. Box 54209, Boulder, CO 80323-4209.

Kidsport, Southern Media Corp., 9625 W. Sample Rd., Coral Springs, FL 33065.

Know Your World Extra, Weekly Reader Corp., 3001 Cindel Dr., Delran, NJ 08370.

Muse, Cobblestone Publishing, Inc., 30 Grove St., Peterborough, NH 03458.

National Geographic World, National Geographic, P.O. Box 2330, Washington, DC 20013.

New Moon Magazine, P.O. Box 3587, Duluth MN 55803.

Odyssey, Cobblestone Publishing, Inc., 30 Grove St., Peterborough, NH 03458.

Owl, Young Naturalist Foundation, 56 The Esplanade, Suite 306, Toronto, Ontario, Canada M5E1A7.

Racing for Kids, Griggs Publishing Co., P.O. Box 500, Concord, NC 28026.

Scholastic Action Magazine, Scholastic, Inc., 2931 E. McCarty St., P.O. Box 3710, Jefferson City, MO 65102.

Scholastic Choices, Scholastic, Inc., 2931 E. McCarty St., P.O. Box 3710, Jefferson City, MO 65102.

Scholastic Math, Scholastic, Inc., 2931 E. McCarty St., P.O. Box 3710, Jefferson City, MO 65102.

Scholastic Search, Scholastic, Inc., 2931 E. McCarty St., P.O. Box 3710, Jefferson City, MO 65102.

Science World, Scholastic, Inc., 2931 E. McCarty St., P.O. Box 3710, Jefferson City, MO 65102.

Skipping Stones: A Multicultural Magazine for Kids, Skipping Stones Magazine, P.O. Box 3939, Eugene, OR 97403.

Spider, Carus Publishing, P.O. Box 7468, Red Oak, IA 51591.

Sports Illustrated for Kids, Sports Illustrated, P.O. Box 60001, Tampa, FL 33660-0001.

Teen Beat, Sterling/McFadden Partnership, 233 Park Ave. S., 6th Floor, New York, NY 10003.

Teen Times, Future Homemakers of America, Inc., 1910 Association Dr., Reston, VA 22091.

TG Magazine, 202 Cleveland St., Toronto, Ontario, Canada M4S2W6.

Thrasher Magazine, High Speed Productions, Inc., 1303 Underwood, P.O. Box 884570, San Francisco, CA 94124.

Time for Kids, Time, Inc., Time & Life Building, 1271 Avenue of the Americas, New York, NY 10020-1393.

3-2-1 Contact, 3-2-1 Contact, P.O. Box 51177, Boulder, CO 80322.

*U*S* Kids*, Carus Publishing, P.O. Box 7468, Red Oak, IA 51591.

Voices of Youth, Communications Publishing Group, Inc., 106 West 11th St., Suite 250, Kansas City, MO 64105.

The Wall Street Journal Classroom Edition, Wall Street Journal, P.O. Box 300, Princeton, NJ 08543.

Weekly Reader: News For Kids, 200 First Standford Place, P.O. Box 120023, Stamford, CT 06912-0023.

Wild West, 602 South King Street, Suite 300, Leesburg, VA 22075.

Wildlife Conservation, 185th St. & Southern Blvd., Bronx, NY 10460.

Young Voices, Young Voices, P.O. Box 2321, Olympia, WA 98507.

Zillions: The Consumer Reports for Kids, Zillions Department, P.O. Box 51777, Boulder, CO 80321.

Bibliography

Blume, J. 1972. *Tales of a Fourth-Grade Nothing*. New York: Dell.

Cambourne, B. 1988. *The Whole Story*. New York: Scholastic.

Canfield, J., and M. V. Hansen. 1993. *Chicken Soup for the Soul*. Deerfield Beach, FL: Health Communications.

———. 1994. *Concise Columbia Encyclopedia*, 3d ed. New York: Columbia University Press.

Dillard, A. 1989. *The Writing Life*. New York: Harper & Row.

Eisner, Elliot W. 1991. *The Enlightened Eye*. New York: Macmillan.

Elbow. P. 1981. *Writing with Power*. New York: Oxford.

Fox, Mem. 1993. *Radical Reflections*. New York: Harcourt Brace.

Gardner, H. 1993. *Frames of Mind*. New York: Basic Books.

Graves, D. H. 1983. *Writing: Teachers and Children at Work*. Portsmouth, NH: Heinemann.

Harvey, S. 1998. *Nonfiction Matters: Reading, Writing, and Research in Grades 3–8*. Portland, ME: Stenhouse.

Harvey, S., and A. Goudvis. 2000. *Strategies That Work: Teaching Comprehension to Enhance Understanding*. Portland, ME: Stenhouse.

Hindley, J. 1996. *In the Company of Children*. Portland, ME: Stenhouse.

King, Stephen. 2000. *On Writing: A Memoir of the Craft*. New York: Scribner.

Kohn, A. 2000. *A Case Against Standardized Testing: Raising the Scores, Ruining the Schools*. Portsmouth, NH: Heinemann.

Neufeldt, V., ed. 1991. *Webster's New World Dictionary*, 3d ed. New York: Simon & Schuster.

Routman, R. 1996. *Literacy at the Crossroads*. Portsmouth, NH: Heinemann.

Saunders, Sylvia. 2001. "Backlash Building Against State Tests." *New York Teacher*, June 6, p. 4.

Smith, F. 1982. *Writing and the Writer*. New York: Holt, Rinehart, and Winston.

Woolridge, Susan. 1997. *Poemcrazy*. New York: Three Rivers Press.

Vygotsky, L. 1978. *Mind and Society*. Cambridge, MA: Harvard University Press.

Also available from Stenhouse

The Writing Lives of Children
Dan Madigan and Victoria T. Koivu-Rybicki

How do children choose the topics they write about? Is their goal of writing to achieve a certain level of literacy, or are they accomplishing something more personal and social? Can a child's writing really be political? How does a child's social and physical environment influence her writing?

The answers are as different and as complex as the children Dan Madigan and Vicki Rybicki reveal in this compelling study of third- and fourth-grade writers in an inner-city school. The ten children they portray have discovered that writing is another way to express their lives, explore their ideas, and define the world about them. In many ways, they are like children in any classroom, but there is a difference. These children have space and time and a forum in which to present their writing. This atmosphere of encouragement and an attentive, thoughtful audience of their peers are the support they need and use to grow as articulate, thoughtful writers.

Why Workshop?
Changing Course in 7–12 English
Edited by Richard Bullock

Why Workshop? offers English and Language Arts teachers in grades 7 through 12 sound advice on using writing and reading workshops as the primary organization of their classrooms. The book's nine essays are written by experienced teachers who are making their teaching work day by day. In the process they give a good mix of testimonials, specific methods, and real-life results. The contributors offer both overviews of workshop teaching and focused essays on specific elements of workshop. An appendix provides an outline of a sample classroom structure based on workshop teaching, with specifics on organizing in terms of the year, the semester, the quarter, the week, and the period. It includes forms for students and letters for parents, assessment tools, and all the basic information one teacher used in creating a workshop teaching environment.

Portfolios in the Classroom
Tools for Learning and Instruction
Beth Schipper and Joanne Rossi

The wonderful effect of the portfolio process is the self-awareness that is activated when kids generate their own selection criteria, make decisions, and reflect on their work. Discussing what they want to include in their portfolio and why, and analyzing which piece of writing or project meets those criteria create connections to learning far beyond the scope of traditional forms of assessment.

Portfolios also increase learning because students take responsibility for their learning, actively engage in the learning process, and grow in confidence and self-esteem. Using examples from real portfolios and successful classroom experiences, Beth Schipper and Joanne Rossi take you step-by-step through helping children create portfolios that reveal accurate assessments of their own work. Beth and Joanne also outline instructional ideas that extend your use of portfolios, provide reproducible forms for you and your students to use, and show you how portfolios can be a tool for parental involvement.

The Author's Profile
Assessing Writing in Context
Teri Beaver

The Author's Profile is a step-by-step tool that you and your students can use to assess their narrative and expository writing. Teri Beaver has developed a set of rubrics that allow a teacher to assess, all on one page, the tools an author has used and the developmental level achieved for each. Each rubric is designed for several pieces of writing, making it possible to see improvement from assignment to assignment. The rubrics also carry brief descriptions on the page for each developmental level of each tool, indicating for an author exactly what may be done to achieve the next level. No longer will a student writer need to ask, "What should I have done to get an A?"

Revising & Editing
Using Models and Checklists to Promote Successful Writing Experiences
Les Parsons

Revising & Editing shows classroom teachers how to address the direct teaching of specific revising and editing skills. Les Parsons clears up the confusion between these two terms that are often used interchangeably. He explores the concept and the goal behind these two distinct practices with specific classroom activities illustrated with student samples. Based on extensive classroom experience, the book includes a host of concrete ways to motivate young writers to improve their work.

Drawing on a wealth of models, checklists, and guidelines, teachers will be able to promote successful writing experiences for fiction and nonfiction. He includes activities encourage students to rethink the writing from initial idea to final product and a tool kit of reproducibles that focus on a range of writing skills.

**www.stenhouse.com
or your local distributor**